D0463850

CONTENTS

To the memory of my father,
Carl Hemphill, who loved me into the kingdom
and taught me to love my Father's kingdom.

Also to the memory of Lewis Drummond,
who developed a passion in me
to spread the kingdom through
my personal witness.

and

To my mentors in ministry,
Mark Corts, Jimmy Draper, and Charles Fuller,
who taught me by word and example how to grow a
kingdom-focused church.

Also to C. F. D. Moule,
my doctrinal supervisor at Cambridge
University who modeled piety and scholarship
during my academic days.

EMPOWERING KINGDOM GROWTH

EKG

THE HEARTBEAT
OF
GOD

KEN HEMPHILL

BROADMAN
&HOLMAN
PUBLISHERS

Nashville, Tennessee

Copyright © 2004
by Ken Hemphill
All rights reserved
Printed in the United States of America

0–8054–3147–0

Published by Broadman & Holman Publishers
Nashville, Tennessee

Dewey Decimal Classification: 231.72
Subject Heading: KINGDOM OF GOD—GROWTH

Scripture quotations are taken from the Holman Christian Standard
Bible® Copyright © 1999, 2000, 2002, 2004 by Holman Bible
Publishers. Used by permission. Italic in biblical text has been added
by the author for emphasis.

1 2 3 4 5 6 7 8 9 10   10 09 08 07 06 05 04

ACKNOWLEDGMENTS

THE WRITING OF THIS BOOK has been one of the most life-changing experiences that I have known. If the message impacts no one but me, it will have been worth the labor. It is my prayer that you will hear the Father calling you to be a kingdom person. I have never had a more profound sense of the Father's daily supervision than I have had during the writing of this book. Anything of value that comes from this book should bring glory to the Father alone.

Any book project is a team effort and this one is no exception. I want to thank my Southern Baptist family who has given me opportunities to serve them in several different capacities. I am particularly indebted to Morris Chapman and Jimmy Draper, who issued the challenge to become the national strategist for *Empowering Kingdom Growth.* I am humbled to be part of a denomination that is willing to refocus its energy by daring to ask the question, "Are we a kingdom people?"

I greatly appreciate the convention-elected task force for their confidence in and support of my efforts on behalf of our denomination. Members of the task force are John Avant, Don Beall, Morris H. Chapman, William O. (Bill) Crews, Carlisle Driggers, David Hankins, John Hays, O. Wyndell Jones, Anthony L. Jordan, Steve Little, James Merritt, Jerry A. Rankin, Robert E. (Bob) Reccord, and J. Robert White.

I am grateful to my Southwestern Seminary family who supported my service as president of that great institution for nine years and encouraged me when I felt God leading me to this new initiative. I appreciate the generosity of the trustees in allowing me to use sabbatical time to complete this study. I will always be indebted to my Southwestern colleagues.

I have been blessed to work with Lifeway Christian Resources and its publishing division, Broadman & Holman, in all the resources God has called me to provide for the edification of the church. Ken Stephens and his entire team have demonstrated great enthusiasm for this project. This is the second project that I have had the pleasure of working with Lawrence Kimbrough. Words will never adequately express my appreciation for his great writing gifts. You would appreciate his work if you were ever allowed to see the difference between my draft and the finished product.

Paula remains my co-laborer in the ministry. This book is in many ways a joint project. Not only did she listen patiently as I preached through this material so many times that she could lip sync many of the messages, but she also provided numerous helpful insights. My girls and their husbands remain a constant source of pleasure as they seek to be kingdom-focused persons. Thank you, Brett and Kristina Boesch, Trey and Rachael Oswald, and Daniel and Katie Banks. Your dad loves you deeply.

This book is dedicated to six men who helped shape my life and ministry. But in truth it is dedicated to you the reader and to the local church. It is my passion that the Lord will use this humble effort to revitalize churches so that they would join the Father in his triumphant kingdom work, until all the nations know him as King.

INTRODUCTION

WHAT IS THE KINGDOM OF GOD?

And what does it mean to be a kingdom person?

There was a time in my life when I might have been tempted to approach these (or perhaps dismiss these) as purely doctrinal questions. I might have considered them valuable items for study, good sermon material, or nice topics of spiritual conversation.

But in the last few years especially, these questions have begun to consume me. They have changed the way I live. They have reached into every single area of my life, leaving nothing untouched, transforming even the most ordinary transactions of my day into opportunities charged with meaning and potential. They have exposed for me the draining, confining nature of modern life and have led me into a daily experience of God's freedom, patience, peace, and perspective.

In the kingdom of God, I have found something far superior to personal fulfillment. I have found the heart of God. I have found my reason for being here.

And I know I'm not alone in thinking this.

It seems that everywhere I turn, I am seeing books and articles about the kingdom of God. Missions agencies are sending out fund-raising letters with an emphasis on the kingdom. Various evangelical denominations have inserted kingdom language into their purpose statements. I am being challenged from many different quarters to build a kingdom family, to look at my calendar and my checkbook with a kingdom focus, and to establish the priorities of my life based on the kingdom of God.

And that's good because these kingdom questions are among the most important a Christian will ever face. Few are more necessary; few are more crucial to our understanding of why we're here and what we should be doing with the years God has left to us on earth.

In many ways these questions defy full, complete answers. This is both the frustration and the beauty in them—frustrating, in that the kingdom of God is too cosmic and complex to be grasped by mere mortals, yet beautiful, in that the kingdom's sheer immensity removes all limits on what God can do through us.

Unlike anything else in life, God's kingdom has absolutely no boundaries. It's not like a television season which, when it comes to an end, must resort to showing tired reruns as a way of maintaining our interest.

It's not like a Saturday afternoon football game that keeps us on the edge of our seats through four exciting quarters only to suddenly come to an end, leaving us descending the bleachers with our empty popcorn boxes and hot dog wrappers, disappointed that there isn't any more.

No, the kingdom of God is big and broad and beyond our wildest imaginations. Its fullness can never be attained. Its resources are never depleted. Its season is never over.

You never get the feeling you've seen all this before.

Yet even in saying this, even while admitting that the kingdom is indeed vast and unsearchable, God in his grace and wisdom has somehow made it simple for us. Honestly, the kingdom of God can be adequately understood just by realizing that he is our King and we are his people, that he is our Master and we are his servants, that he sets the rules and we simply obey.

But while this is simple in theory, of course, it is not so easy in practice.

And so, whether considering either the kingdom's eternal mysteries or its basic, everyday opportunities, we realize that we are confronted with issues bigger than we are. Knowing what truly ignites the heart of God is something we desperately need to understand, yet we have such a hard time defining it. We don't always know it when we see it. We don't always live by it when we do. And we don't always recognize it when we're missing it.

Therefore, we are brought to our knees, where we must always be if we are ever truly to understand the kingdom and its implications in our lives.

Here, then, we begin—in humility and openness, in silence and worship—the only way we can approach God and expect to hear his voice.

COME AS YOU ARE

Any time we believers open ourselves to a new way of thinking that can lead us closer to Christ and deeper into our life's purpose, the enemy always moves in to counteract our zeal for discovery, to weaken our hunger for change. That's why, since God has led you to this book, you may find yourself fighting off temptations designed to keep you from embracing this kingdom message.

For example, you may feel too empty at this point in your life to give God much to work with. That's OK. God's kingdom often finds its most fertile ground in the hearts of those who are tired and spent. The Bible is filled with examples of men and women God met at their thirstiest . . . and led them to streams of living water.

Feeling guilty? Disillusioned, perhaps? Frustrated by the fact that, if it's taken you this long to get here, it's probably too late to start trying? You're never too late to begin seeking afresh the kingdom of God. Anything as powerful as God's irreversible march through eternity is strong enough to animate any given day, week, or month in a believer's life.

Feeling as though your days are too few to matter? *All* of our days are few, whether we realize it or not. We'd be shocked if we really understood how small a speck even a full lifetime is in the span of eternity. But the things God can do through us in the space of six months, or sixty years, or whatever amount of time we are allowed to give him on earth, is more than any of us can begin to predict. The past is done. The rest is . . . who knows, when it's placed in his hands?

Whatever your situation, wherever you are, however you feel about yourself and your relationship with God at this moment in life, now is the time to ask the Lord what it would mean for you to be a kingdom person.

And to get ready for the adventure of a lifetime.

How Do We Get There from Here?

The journey we are about to undertake will cover a lot of familiar ground as we travel the pages of the Bible in search of

God's kingdom. This is the way it should be. We are not inventing a new model or lifestyle here but building on what God has already shown us, mining it out of our own backyard, fully aware that what God is revealing to us in these days are truths that have always been part of who we are.

That's because the kingdom has always been. The kingdom has been God's plan and purpose for all eternity, and he has painted its colors from one corner of the Scripture to the other—sometimes in muted shades; sometimes in bold, visible designs.

Therefore, we see God's kingdom best not by listening to someone like me devising some elaborate system of thought but by opening our Bibles and letting God speak to us through the pages of his story, through the lives of his people, and through the love of his Son.

The kingdom has always been central to our relationship with God, for it has always been his means of relating to us. His purpose has always been to raise up a people who would embrace his mission, embody his name, and obey his Word.

And we are that people, connected across time with God's people of every age, united with him and with one another in living out his eternal message.

So while this book is certainly biblical in nature, format, and setup, it remains—like the Bible itself—practical and ready-made for real life. These thirty chapters are a long way from being heady discussions that are largely disconnected from life on the ground. Certainly, the kingdom does possess a great deal of spiritual, eternal, doctrinal reasons for being, but this doesn't disqualify it from having a huge bearing on every day, every moment, and every encounter of our lives. In fact, its eternal nature is what gives the kingdom its application to this very hour. Should not the things that will matter most for eternity be the things that should matter most to us right now?

Yes, God's kingdom lives. We live in *it,* and it lives through *us.*

THE KINGDOM QUEST

I am so glad you have chosen to come along on this exploration of the kingdom, to place yourself, your family, and your church into the vast ocean of opportunity which kingdom living, and kingdom living alone, provides.

The kingdom of God is a biblical theme transformational enough to make big changes in your life. To live in the kingdom will likely require you to alter your perspectives on a lot of the things you do. It could possibly mean a relocation to another city or country, a job change, or some other major decision or event in your life. (It has for me.) It could possibly mean a new way of thinking about the way you spend your free time. It will definitely open your eyes to the people you come into contact with on a regular basis and the veiled importance of each moment of your day. It will help you find great value in the once-incidental aspects of life and will give you the rightful feeling that you're involved in something that will outlast and outlive you.

In short, the kingdom of God is an exciting, life-changing way to live and to serve. It will impact every area of your personal life:

- You will listen to the news and read the paper with a new perspective.
- You will view the events of daily life with a kingdom focus.

- Standing in line at the checkout counter will no longer be a humdrum waste of time but potentially a kingdom opportunity.
- You will view with different eyes the financial and time resources at your disposal.
- You will begin to ask, "How can I use my home for kingdom purposes?"
- Your time at work and play will take on new meaning.
- You will be motivated to do your job with even greater excellence.
- You will begin raising your children with an eye on how to best prepare them for life in the kingdom, instilling in them the kingdom principles that will position them ever at Christ's command.

Much is at stake if we fail to grasp the meaning of the kingdom for us:

- We will fail to understand what is most important to our Lord, what was on the heart of God from before the creation of the world.
- We will fail to see God's kingdom activity all around us.
- We will fail to enjoy the privilege of participating in supernatural work.
- We will fail to employ the available power of the Holy Spirit.
- We will miss the joy of knowing that we have been pleasing to our Father.

- We will miss the exhilarating freedom that comes from radical obedience.
- We will miss the opportunity to experience God's abundant provision and will continue to be plagued by worry, fear, and anxiety.
- Saddest of all, we will miss God's purpose for our lives.

When I think about what kingdom living could mean for you, your family, and your church, I am excited. When I think about the change it could bring about in your local community, I am hopeful. When I think about the impact such faithful obedience to God's Word could have on our world, I am overwhelmed. You are an instrument in the hand of the sovereign God of the universe.

To live with this kind of kingdom focus is not merely one viable choice among a long list of priority-setting options and life-management techniques. For the believer in Christ, living in the kingdom is the only reality there is. To "seek first the kingdom" is to have all these other things "provided for you" (Matt. 6:33).

The kingdom of God is everything.

And living in the kingdom is God's purpose for you. And for me. And for all of God's people.

SECTION 1

A King and His People

Chapter 1

KINGDOM MOMENTS

Jerusalem, all Judea, and all the vicinity of the Jordan were flocking to him.

MATTHEW 3:5

IF YOU'RE ONE OF THOSE who thinks God could certainly find someone more qualified than you are to do his work . . . if you're not sure you have the right style of dress or the right words to say . . . if you don't feel impressive or talented enough to represent Christ very well . . . I need to hook you back up with an old friend of yours.

John.

John the Baptist, you remember, appears unexpectedly on the biblical scene, wearing his garment of camel hair tucked in by a leather belt around his waist. The only other noticeable aspect about him was his eating habits. His appetite for wild honey doesn't sound all that bad, but his preference for locusts doesn't leave much to the imagination. I know our modern germ-fighting culture is a far cry from the cleanliness and hygiene of the average first-century citizen, but I have a feeling John was revolting even by the standards of his own generation.

Yet *something* was drawing the crowds to him, and I seriously doubt it was the camel hair robe! Matthew 3:5 tells us that

"Jerusalem, all Judea, and all the vicinity of the Jordan were flocking to him."

Certainly not everyone in a crowd of this size was coming out of sheer curiosity. Perhaps some were. Neither were they coming to hear a polished orator. In fact, much of what he had to say was harsh and offensive, especially to those who were the most certain they already had their religious act together.

No, John wasn't afraid to speak his mind. But he basically had just this one message: "Repent, because the kingdom of heaven has come near!" (Matt. 3:2).

The Bible reader is given no prelude to this "kingdom of heaven" terminology, no elaborate explanation to help us understand what John meant by this seemingly cryptic message. Nowhere in the Old Testament will you find the "kingdom of heaven" or the "kingdom of God" written in precisely these words.

Yet many in John's audience apparently had some level of understanding about this—enough of an idea, at least, to know that the "kingdom of heaven" was worth repenting of their sins. Plenty of people were doing repenting, coming to be baptized, wanting to prepare themselves for the coming of this kingdom, for the coming of this King.

This was a kingdom moment. And John was right in the middle of it.

Now God could have used anybody to make this announcement. We'd expect he might have chosen someone with a little more gentility and sophistication, someone who'd more naturally appeal to the masses, someone more appropriate to herald such earth-shattering news.

But God had his eye on a tough-bearded wilderness man, someone he knew would embrace his mission, embody his name, and obey his Word.

Locusts and all, John still had all the makings of a kingdom person.

So can we.

ANOTHER KINGDOM MOMENT

The kingdom arrived in full display, of course, when Jesus stepped to the waters of the Jordan to be baptized by John. Pointing him out to the crowd, John said, "This is the One I told you about: 'After me comes a man who has surpassed me, because He existed before me'" (John 1:30).

It was clear that this man, Jesus, was the one who had come to inaugurate the kingdom—a kingdom that had always been but was now being personified in the face of Christ. His kingdom would hold reward for many—to those who would respond to his message, to those whom he would baptize "with the Holy Spirit and fire" and gather like "wheat into the barn." Yet because the kingdom of God would come with a call for human response, not all would be included in the blessing of his reign. Indeed there would be a great number to be burned in a "fire that never goes out" (Matt. 3:11–12).

This kingdom would have an impact on everyone, whether they wanted it to or not! Indeed, it has always sparked a battle.

One of the biggest, in fact, happened right off the bat.

Immediately after Jesus' baptism the Spirit led him into the wilderness to be tested by the devil, to reveal under heavy assault the power and authority of the Son of God. To claim his kingdom.

The devil, the arch adversary of God, "took Him up and showed Him all the kingdoms of the world in a moment of time"—a height and depth of authority, the devil said, which had been "given over to me, and I can give it to anyone I want" (Luke 4:5–6).

Much was at stake here. Satan had indeed been bestowed temporary dominion over the earth. Jesus himself would later refer to him as the "ruler of this world," even though in the same breath he would pronounce Satan's soon and certain defeat (John 12:31).

With so much riding on Jesus' entrance into the world to redeem lost humanity, Satan went for the jugular, offering Jesus the easy way to world dominion. No cross. No blood. No crown of thorns or a lash across the back. *Just worship me! This one time!*

This one time!

It would have been easy to argue that the ends might have justified the means. But the issue for the Son was not a shortcut to success but loyalty to the Father, a loyalty that has but one appropriate response: absolute obedience.

So when Jesus declared his intention to worship and serve the Lord alone, a direct quote from God's instructions to his people thousands of years before (Deut. 6:13), he was choosing the kingdom of God and the reward of the Father over the kingdoms of the world and all their flashy yet fleeting glory.

And we, his followers, face this same decision every day. Do we desire the kingdom of God or the kingdoms of this world? Will it be personal fame or the Father's glory?

So in Jesus we see another distinguishing characteristic of a kingdom person.

A CONTINUOUS KINGDOM MOMENT

When Jesus strode into the world from the wilderness of temptation, he did so with a message. This is how the Gospel writers remembered it: "From then on Jesus began to preach, 'Repent, because the kingdom of heaven has come near'" (Matt. 4:17)—a message perfectly consistent with that of John the Baptist, indeed with the entire history of God's dealing with his people.

This little phrase "began to preach" is so important because it indicates that this was not only Jesus' inaugural message; it was his ongoing message. In fact, when we fast-forward to the last days and hours of Jesus' life on earth, after his death and his resurrection, we see him with his disciples, having "presented Himself alive to them by many convincing proofs, appearing to them during 40 days and *speaking about the kingdom of God*" (Acts 1:3).

Seeing that Jesus both began and ended his earthly ministry by teaching on the same theme, we can only conclude that the kingdom was of critical importance to him and that he desired his followers then, as well as his followers of every age, to know and to share this central reality.

James Stewart, in his classic book *The Life and Teaching of Jesus Christ,* captured the significance of this message well.

> Every new idea that has ever burst upon the world
> has had a watchword. Always there has been some word
> or phrase in which the very genius of the thing has been
> concentrated and focused, some word or phrase to
> blazon on its banners when it went marching out into
> the world, . . . something to wave like a flag, to rally the

ranks, and win recruits. The greatest idea that has ever been born upon the earth is the Christian idea. And Christianity came with a watchword, magnificent and mighty and imperial; and the watchword was, "The kingdom of God."[1]

This one phrase, the "kingdom of God," occurs more than one hundred times in the Gospels alone. And even when it is not spoken in so many words, the importance of the kingdom is implied in everything Jesus said and did.

It should be the same with us. Our awareness of God's grand mission and purpose, the advancing of his kingdom, should swallow and absorb every second of our lives. This doesn't mean we're always in church. It doesn't mean we do nothing but pray and read our Bibles. It doesn't mean we never get to watch television or go shopping or rest after a long day's work. But even in these ordinary activities of the day, our lives are at the command of Christ, our desires and affections are in his hand, and our minds are alert to whatever he wants us to see and hear and learn and do.

From first to last, from sunup to sundown, from now until the end, it is the kingdom of God—God's rule, God's reign, God's reward.

Always. All the time.

What Is the Kingdom?

OK, now is the time to go ahead and establish an early, working definition of what we mean by the "kingdom of God."

Most everyone agrees that the kingdom refers to the rule and reign of God. This is an eternal reality—a rule that has always existed, a reign that will exist forever—yet God has established his kingdom on earth, which gives it a present-tense aspect, as well. Jesus, you remember, spoke often of the *future* dimension of his kingdom, when "many will come from east and west, and recline at the table with Abraham, Isaac, and Jacob in the kingdom of heaven" (Matt. 8:11). Yet he could also say, with equal accuracy, that "if I drive out demons by the finger of God, then the kingdom of God has come to you" (Luke 11:20). This absolute, unrivaled, thorough control of God over all things, which will one day be visibly seen for the reality it is, has already invaded our day and time. And we celebrate what we cannot see by choosing to live in the predawn light of forever . . . right now.

God rules us. We are his. He orchestrates events and directs human history, while somehow—somehow—leaving intact our ability to make decisions and choose our own path. We walk into each day fully aware by faith that every person we see, every article we read, and every question we are asked are all coming our way by the intention of the King. Wrapped inside each of these events is an opportunity for us to embrace his mission, embody his name, and obey his Word—to live in concert with his rightful rule over our lives.

This is God's kingdom at work in our day.

This is our ongoing opportunity to walk in continual kingdom moments.

Historically, we can think of the kingdom as occurring in four unbroken time periods:

1. *The Old Testament.* Under the old covenant, Israel was to function as the people of God—the subjects of the King—used by him to display his love, mercy,

and glory with the expressed purpose of reaching the nations.

2. *Jesus' life.* The long-awaited promise of a coming King—a Messiah, a Redeemer—became a living, breathing reality through Jesus' earthly ministry. He himself was God's kingdom in the flesh.

3. *The church.* The church is not the equivalent of the kingdom, but ever since Christ's ascension—and until he comes again—the church is God's primary instrument for kingdom advance in the world.

4. *Christ's return.* The final, unending phase of the kingdom will begin when the triumphant King returns for his bride. "He will reign forever and ever!" (Rev. 11:15), "and His kingdom will have no end" (Luke 1:33).

We are going to cover this grand sweep of God's kingdom in much more detail in the chapters ahead because I want you to see that this kingdom has been God's perpetual purpose from day one. I want you to see the size and weight and enormity of his rule and reign. I want you to get a taste of the freedom and excitement that arise from being a daily part of God's eternal plan.

I want you to be a kingdom person . . . in this kingdom moment.

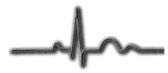 *The United States is the world's third largest nation in population with 290 million people. Only China and India have more people. Of the 290 million people in the United States, an*

estimated 213 million are lost. If only the lost population were considered, the United States would be the fourth largest country behind China, India, and Indonesia. (Source: NAMB)

- Where do you see the kingdom of God today?
- What has happened to Jesus' message of repentance in our society?
- Do you know someone you would label a "kingdom person"?

Chapter 2

GOD TO THE RESCUE

**You have seen what I did to the Egyptians and how I carried
you on eagles' wings and brought you to Me.**

EXODUS 19:4

"WHERE DO WE START?"

Have you ever asked yourself this question just before undertaking a daunting task—like cleaning out your attic, or planning
your Thanksgiving dinner, or creating a family budget in the
hopes of finding a little money left over?

Or perhaps worst of all—when packing for a move.

We recently moved from the president's home at
Southwestern Baptist Seminary in Fort Worth, Texas, to a lovely
condominium in Hendersonville, Tennessee. As you might imagine, we had a little bit more space in our former home than we do
in our new place of abode. Not everything that fit so nicely and
comfortably into our previous residence found the same kind of
room in our new condo.

So in the process of this move, I discovered one of the undeniable truths of life: "Stuff will always expand to fill its available
space." And when you challenge your stuff to squeeze into a more
confining environment, there's not much choice but to let the
stuff go and let the environment win.

We knew this, of course, and had prepared ourselves accordingly. We had thrown a lot of stuff away already. We had given away scads of clothes and books. We had thinned down considerably and thought we were in pretty good shape to move into our new, smaller home.

But the day after the movers had deposited the last of our belongings into our Tennessee condo—despite our best efforts at making this as simple as possible—the rooms were absolutely filled with boxes. And we found ourselves asking the same question I'm asking myself now in thinking through the material for this book:

"Where am I going to put all this stuff?"

In trying to articulate the scope of God's redemptive history and his purpose for his people, a writer is left with an exciting yet enormous task. *This kingdom of his is huge!* How does a person make it fit into their lives, much less into a single book?

So to help make this more manageable, I've applied a few other things I learned from our recent move:

1. *Even a daunting task is made easier if you take it a little bit at a time.* That's why I've decided to unpack this material slowly, delivering it to you in short chapters.

2. *It's best to start at the beginning.* Before we could even begin to unpack our boxes, we had to get the first things in place—the beds, the furniture, the major appliances. And so in this book I'm also going to start at the beginning, with the first biblical mention of the kingdom, found in a pivotal passage from Exodus 19. This is where we will begin our journey.

OUT OF EGYPT

The focal passage of this chapter—Exodus 19:1–6—begins with a time line: "In the third month, on the same day of the month that the Israelites had left the land of Egypt, they entered the Wilderness of Sinai."

We all know the events that led the Israelites up to this point. God had been building and uniting his people from the beginning of time, through the entire account of Genesis and his dealings with Abraham, Isaac, Jacob, and Joseph; through Israel's descent into slavery in Egypt; and through the undeniable deliverance of his people from the hand of Pharaoh.

At the beginning of Exodus 19, that day of liberation was now three months past. To the day.

By this time they were in the rough, rocky, virtually uninhabited region of Sinai. I can assure you, they had not been drawn here because of the travel brochures, the golf courses, and the luxurious accommodations. They had been brought here on the wings of a promise—a promise made by God to Moses from the audible branches of the burning bush: "This will be the sign to you that I have sent you: when you bring the people out of Egypt, you will all worship God at this mountain" (Exod. 3:12).

So Moses had been drawn to this place the same way a magnet draws iron filings. He wanted to experience Yahweh's presence just as he had at the burning bush. He wanted his brethren to know the life-giving presence of the God of Abraham, Isaac, and Jacob.

This was not just any day. This was a day so sovereignly ordered by God that it fell on "the same day of the month" as the day they had dragged their families, their belongings, and four hundred years of backbreaking history out of the slave pits of Egypt. Moses had only one item on his agenda this day: a meeting with God.

So while all the people were camped at the base of the mountain, Moses made his way up the rocky face and into the presence of God. And when he reached his appointed location, the Lord gave him a message for the people.

The message essentially had three parts:

1. *I delivered you from the Egyptians.* You'll remember that Pharaoh was not eager to release his slaves and wasn't shaken by Moses' demand to let the people of God go free. The Egyptians had a pantheon of gods—among them, Pharaoh himself. So in a cosmic showdown, God had sent a series of plagues aimed right at the Egyptian gods—one blight and bad thing after another—up to and including the death of the firstborn children of Egypt.

The Israelites' release, then, was in no way a grant of amnesty by the goodwill of the Egyptian government. Their release was sprung by the hand of Almighty God.

God, of course, had his reasons for doing this, even for using an unwitting instrument like Pharaoh to work his sovereign plan. Listen to his words directed at Pharaoh: "I have let you live for this purpose: to show you My power *and to make My name known in all the earth*" (Exod. 9:16). Even at the miraculous crossing of the Red Sea, God's purpose had been to "receive glory by means of Pharaoh, all his army, and his chariots and horsemen. The Egyptians will know that I am the Lord when I receive glory through [them]" (Exod. 14:17–18).

Don't miss this. It is vitally important.

God had delivered his people from Egypt to demonstrate his power and to give them a global impact. He had chosen them to "make [his] name known in all the earth."

The Israelites had been eyewitnesses and recipients of God's redemptive power. By delivering them from bondage, he had revealed his absolute control over nature, over Egypt, and over all the Egyptian gods. Throughout the Old Testament, generation after generation of Israel would look back on this one event as the pivotal event in their salvation history.

God himself had delivered them.

2. *I carried you on eagles' wings.* This imagery not only speaks of God's deliverance but also of his presence and provision. The eagle, of course, is a bird of great majesty and strength. Can't you just picture God soaring high over his people as they made their treacherous way to Sinai, guarding them from predators, spotting danger in all directions, providing them the safety of his powerful protection? And during those times when the journey became unbearable and they could hardly put one foot in front of the other, this majestic eagle would swoop down and bear them up on his wings.

This powerful image of God's provision and protection so impressed Moses that he used it as a key element in his great song of deliverance recorded in Deuteronomy 32: "He watches over His nest like an eagle and hovers over His young; He spreads His wings, catches him, and lifts him up on His pinions" (vv. 11–12). God had not only redeemed Israel but had personally nurtured them as they journeyed to the place where he had promised to meet with them.

3. *I brought you to myself.* This third phrase may be the most intimate of all. This was no distant, impersonal God speaking. He

was instead a God of love who had redeemed his people and cared for their every need. More than this, he had remained with them each step of the way, permitting them to experience him through worship.

He not only wanted them safe; he wanted them with *him*.

It was probably difficult for the children of Israel to believe that the God of creation, the invisible God who had sustained Abraham, Isaac, and Jacob, and who now spoke to Moses on the mountaintop, truly desired to have a personal relationship with them.

But he did. Oh, how he did!

And oh, how he still wants a personal relationship with his people today!

THE OFFER STILL STANDS

I have the privilege of visiting many churches across America, a joy and delight I never take for granted. I have preached in their pulpits and have talked to their members. So this statement I'm about to make, as bold and dangerous as it may be to say, is not a wild idea but an in-the-trenches observation:

It is possible that the reason many church members do not have a kingdom focus is because they do not have a personal relationship with the King.

They have not been redeemed. They are still in Egypt.

Now I'm not just referring to the visitors I've seen in church at someone's invitation. I'm talking about many of those who occupy a pew every week and perhaps serve in some ongoing capacity but who have never received God's redemption for themselves or accepted his covenant offer of salvation. Far too many people still live as if church membership, decency in morals, and whatever else they bring to the table in the way of good works should be enough to satisfy God.

It isn't.

Before the Israelites could become God's unique possession, a member of his royal priesthood, a servant in his kingdom, they first had to let God do something for them that they couldn't do for themselves.

They had to experience God's redemption. There was no other way.

And the same is true for everyone who reads this book. The question of the hour is a simple yet serious one: *do you know for certain that you have a personal, covenant relationship with God?*

Until you do, this kingdom message is going to cause you nothing but frustration.

You Can

For many of you this is well-known news. But if God is dealing with you at this point, and you know in your heart that you have not surrendered your heart and life to Jesus Christ, let me remind you of a few essentials.

1. *Just as Israel found itself in bondage under a cruel Pharaoh, the Bible teaches that all of us are born in bondage to sin.* Romans 3:23 states man's problem very clearly: "For all have sinned and fall short of the glory of God." We were created in God's image and designed to live in relationship with him, but our sin has created a great gulf between us and a holy God.

2. *Yet God has provided us the means of escape.* Paul declares, "For the wages of sin is death, but the gift of God is eternal life in

Christ Jesus our Lord" (Rom. 6:23). This one verse contains both the bad news and the good news of the gospel. Sin has led us into spiritual death, separating us from God. But eternal life in Christ is his gift to us. And just like Israel's deliverance from Egypt, it is an act of God's redemptive grace, a gift that cannot be earned but must be received, a redemption made possible by a precious gift of the covenant God.

"For God loved the world in this way: He gave His only Son, so that everyone who believes in Him will not perish but have eternal life" (John 3:16). Jesus, the perfect Son of God, lived a sinless life and yet was crucified like a common criminal. God the Father "made the One who did not know sin to be sin for us, so that we might become the righteousness of God in Him" (2 Cor. 5:21).

These are all wonderful truths, and you have most likely heard them many times before. But hearing them without truly believing them is not sufficient. Like Israel, we must have firsthand knowledge of God's redemptive work. We must respond to his offer of redemption. We must acknowledge our sinful condition and choose to turn away from it to turn instead toward God, to choose to serve him as our rightful King.

If you have not experienced God's redemptive activity in your life, you can. The Bible says, "If you confess with your mouth 'Jesus is Lord,' and believe in your heart that God raised Him from the dead, you will be saved" (Rom. 10:9).

So if this has made sense to you and if you desire to know God's redemptive work for yourself, ask him to forgive your sin and to enter your heart as Lord and Savior.

Perhaps you could pray something like this: "Father, I know that I have sinned against you. I am sorry for my sin and I turn from it today. I believe that Jesus died for my sin and was raised to give me life. I invite him to come into my heart and to be my personal Savior. It is my desire to join in covenant relationship with you and with your people. Amen."

If you have sincerely prayed this prayer, then you are indeed a child of the living God, a servant in his kingdom. If you are already attending church, you should tell your pastor about what you've experienced. If you're reading this book on your own and have made this decision to follow Christ, be sure to seek out a Christian friend at work or in your neighborhood, or visit a nearby Bible-believing church. You'll want to discover the joy of growing to spiritual maturity together with other believers.

The teaching of the Bible is clear: there must first be redemption before there can be life in the kingdom.

And then . . . everything!

- How does the kingdom of God fit into your current life and lifestyle?
- What would need to change for the kingdom to fit in you life? Would you need to get rid of some things? What? Where will you begin to make a change?

Chapter 3

I WILL IF YOU WILL

**Now if you will listen to Me and carefully keep My covenant,
you will be My own possession out of all the peoples,
although all the earth is Mine.**

EXODUS 19:5

EVERY PARENT UNDERSTANDS the "if, then" phrase.

And all children, if they know what's good for them, understands it, as well.

My mom used the classic: "If you eat all your vegetables, Son, then you can have some dessert." Dad's sounded more like this: "If you get the yard mowed, we'll go to the game tonight."

I quickly got the message that privileges are often preceded by responsibilities. No carrots, no cake. No lawn mower, no night life.

I must be honest with you. There were occasions when I failed to fulfill my stated responsibility and thus missed out on the blessing. It's not that my disobedience caused me to be rejected as a son, but I did miss out on all that was available to me inside of that wonderful relationship.

The people of Israel would have known exactly what I'm talking about.

Most of the so-called gods of Moses' day were seen as tyrannical despots who afflicted men according to the gods' own whims. They arbitrarily called the shots, and the people did their best to keep them happy. These gods were to be appeased, not enjoyed . . . or at least unprovoked. The less notice the gods paid to the people, the better.

That's what made God's promise of covenant with Israel so special, so unprecedented. This God wanted relationship with his people. He was willing to treat them with love, mercy, and grace, to value their worth as his creation, to care about what happened to them.

He wanted them for his own possession, not his own plaything.

He wanted covenant with them.

THE NATURE OF COVENANT

A covenant, you know, is a pact or treaty between two parties of either equal or unequal authority. Though unheard of at this period in history as a way of describing the relationship between the gods and the people, covenants were indeed commonplace in the political and economic agreements of the ancient Near East.

We find numerous examples in the Bible of covenants between two people or between a group of people. Jonathan and David established a *covenant* of friendship. The prophets frequently condemned Israel for the *covenants* they established with foreign nations. The marriage relationship itself is said to be a *covenant* between a man and a woman, with God as their witness.

But God was under no obligation to enter into a covenant relationship with his people. Yet he chose to do so. This is huge—a major, consistent theme of the Bible.

His first covenant had been given to Noah (Gen. 9:9–17). When Noah and his family had emerged from the ark, God promised never to repeat a flood of global proportions. He signified this covenant with a rainbow. In this case the covenant required no human response. It was simply a solemn commitment on the part of holy God.

God also had made a covenant with Abraham (Gen. 12:1–3 and 15:18). He had promised that Abraham's family tree would be a source of blessing to all nations. Once again, the covenant involved divine promises but did not call for human obedience.[1]

Yet on this day at the foot of Mount Sinai, three months after the people's deliverance from Egypt, God told Israel that this unique relationship between the two of them would no longer be one they simply received. It would be a relationship that would either grow and flourish or lag and weaken, based on the way they responded to him.

Exodus 19 is the beginning of a large block of material that extends all the way to Numbers 10. Unlike the chapters before them, when decades and centuries sailed by in a matter of verses, this entire stretch of Scripture is given from God to Moses to the Israelites within a short period of time—days, weeks, months.

And it is rich with covenant.

Three things about this promise demand our special attention.

1. *The obedience required by this covenant was subsequent to Israel's deliverance from bondage.* God was not threatening to send his people back to Egypt. They had already been delivered by his

act of redemptive grace. The obedience prescribed in the covenant would all occur after redemption had already taken place. In the same way, we do not earn our salvation by any work of obedience on our part.

2. *The "if" clause demanded a voluntary response.* God was not coercing Israel to serve him the way a conquering king might have been expected to do. This is a key for understanding the nature of our King and what it means to be a kingdom person. We are not forced to obey, although he warns us in love that our disobedience will cause us unnecessary harm and suffering.

3. *The "if" clause described the appropriate way of responding to God—in gratitude for his deliverance.* Obedience was not a condition of deliverance but a doorway to its fulness. This obedience was motivated by thankfulness for what God had done. It enabled the people to enjoy both their relationship with him and their usefulness in his purpose, to experience everything their redemption had won for them.

Obedience is inseparable from covenant.

OBEDIENCE: THE KEY TO USEFULNESS

Do you remember Jesus' response to the crowd of Jews who wanted to know if he was the Messiah? "How long are you going to keep us in suspense?" they ranted. "If You are the Messiah, tell us plainly" (John 10:24).

Jesus knew there was little point in trying to convince his accusers of his credentials. He knew they wouldn't believe him anyway . . . because they were not his sheep. "My sheep hear My voice," Jesus said. "I know them, and they follow Me" (John 10:27).

"They follow Me." This obedience to God's voice gives clear evidence of covenant relationship. It is the key to covenant identity, usefulness, and enjoyment.

To thrive in God's kingdom, we must obey his every word.

In the books of Exodus and Leviticus, God established the parameters of his covenant relationship with Israel by means of the law—a law of blessing and prosperity, God's prescribed pathway to a holy, productive life.

Unfortunately, however, the Israelites proved to be stubborn children. They continually ignored God's law, treating lightly their place in his kingdom.

Their disobedience came into clear view as they were poised to inhabit the land of promise God had prepared for them. His desire for his covenant people was that they would enjoy this land of milk and honey, that they would thrive in his blessing and demonstrate his power and holiness among the nations. God had promised to give them this land by the strength of his might.

You would think they would have remembered how God had borne them on eagle's wings when Pharaoh's forces had trapped them at the Red Sea. It hadn't even been that long ago!

But you remember the story. The spies were sent out to inspect the land, and they came back with a frightful report, scaring the people to death—scaring the people into disobedience.

And so an entire generation died without having ever accomplished anything of value for God, without having ever enjoyed the unique covenant relationship that was right within their grasp.

All for the lack of faithful obedience.

The book of Deuteronomy follows on the heels of this tragic story—the pointless wanderings of a chosen people. After forty years of waste and regret, Moses restated God's original conditions for the people's covenant usefulness. By recounting Israel's journey, by retelling the story of Israel's recent past, he hoped to teach a new generation the importance of trust and obedience.

If they were going to enjoy the land of promise, Moses told them, obedience would have to pave the way. If they were going to partake in the blessings of kingdom living, faithfulness would have to come first.

Let's listen in on a few of Moses' instructions:

- "Therefore, love the LORD your God and always keep His mandate and His statutes, ordinances, and commands" (Deut. 11:1).

- "Keep every command I am giving you today, so that you may have the strength to cross into and possess the land you are to inherit" (Deut. 11:8).

- "If you carefully obey My commands I am giving you today, to love the LORD your God and serve Him with all your heart and all your soul, I will provide rain for your land in season, the early and late rains, and you will harvest your grain, new wine, and oil. I will provide grass in your fields for your livestock. You will eat and be satisfied" (Deut. 11:13–15).

- "Look, today I set before you a blessing and a curse: there will be a blessing, if you obey the commands of the LORD your God I am giving you today, and a curse, if you do not obey the commands of the LORD your God, and you turn aside from the path I command you today by following other gods you have not known" (Deut. 11:26–28).

COVENANT KEEPER

If we were in a room together and I were to tell you that there were two doors we could go through to exit the room, one door marked "blessing" and the other "cursing," none of us would intentionally stand in line to go through the door marked "cursing."

Yet this is what we do every time we disobey God's Word. We choose "cursing" over "blessing." We choose death over life. We place ourselves in spiritual danger and render our lives ineffective in God's service.

We lose sight of the kingdom.

Again, this doesn't mean that our redemptive relationship with God is conditional, based on our performance. But it does mean that our obedience directly impacts our effectiveness in appropriating God's blessing and in furthering his kingdom through our lives.

God calls on his people to be steadfast. If we couldn't be obedient to him, he wouldn't expect it of us. If we couldn't do what he has said, he wouldn't have said it. Therefore, his "if, then" challenge should greet our ears with a note of encouragement.

Yes, we can keep his covenant.

Yes, we can be productive.

Yes, we can live in the full measure of his kingdom reality.

We know for certain that God will keep his side of the bargain. And we are equally sure that he will give us everything we need in order to hold up our side, as well.

But maybe you haven't been as obedient as you should. And you know it. Maybe you continue to fail the Lord with far too much regularity. Maybe you have experienced so many of the damaging side effects of sin that you doubt you can ever string together a long stretch of faithfulness anymore.

Yes, you can. This covenant still stands. This kingdom still calls to you. This God who promised blessing to the people of Israel stands beside you this very day, drawing you back into fellowship, seeking to restore, promising you freedom in place of failure.

He wants you close. He wants you near him. He wants you to experience the daily fullness of the covenant.

If you've received Christ into your heart by faith, of course, you're saved from the eternal effects of your sin. And that's wonderful! But God has even greater blessings in store for you. And they hang in the balance of your obedience.

Are you willing to confess your disobedience to God and receive his full pardon? First John 1:9 tells us, "If we confess our sins, He is faithful and righteous to forgive us our sins and to cleanse us from all unrighteousness."

And to march us boldly into his kingdom.

Yes, we can.

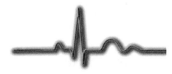

- What evidence do you see that people keep—or fail to keep—covenant relationships with other people today?
- What do you think is required of a person to obey God? Do you know anyone who does this?

- How would our society change if people were obedient to God?
- How would your life change if you were more obedient to God?

Chapter 4

A Movable Possession

**You will be My own possession out of all the peoples,
although all the earth is Mine.**

EXODUS 19:5B

WHO OF US HASN'T SEEN a child draw a treasured toy or blanket to his chest and declare, "Mine!" We understand the sentiment. This possession of his is special. It has a specific use and brings joy to its owner. That's why he guards it with such great passion.

It is a treasured possession.

I mentioned earlier that my wife, Paula, and I recently moved. Because we knew we wanted to downsize, we went into this realizing we would have to part with some of our possessions. But we honestly didn't realize how difficult a task this would be.

Actually, we did a pretty good job of this in the early stages. We had no trouble discarding clothes we hadn't worn in years. In fact, we genuinely enjoyed the prospect of helping those who could profit from our used possessions. We even distributed to others some of our furniture that we knew wouldn't fit inside our new home. Things were going great. This wasn't as bad as we thought.

Then things began to tighten up.

I would pick up some meaningless or useless possession of Paula's. (It seemed meaningless from *my* vantage point, at least.) As I would cast it into the giveaway pile, she would rush to its rescue, explaining to me why this item had such special meaning. Often it was sentimental in nature, but nonetheless we discovered (both of us) that we have a real attachment to our possessions. They have purpose. They give us joy.

Would it surprise you, then, to learn that you too are a special possession to God—that you have both meaning and purpose to him? That you bring him joy?

This is what God said to Israel. They had not been redeemed, you'll recall, for the sole purpose of escaping the bondage of slavery. God hadn't done all he wanted to do through them once they had passed the "Now Leaving Egypt" signs on their way out of town. No, God had a larger plan in mind for them—a *much* larger plan. They were to be a part of his strategy to reach the nations.

They were to be the prized possessions of his kingdom.

And so are we. We have not been saved merely to be rescued from hell and guaranteed a home in heaven. God has a much larger plan in store for us.

We are his special possessions.

THE BIRTH OF A NATION

A quick look back will help us see this more clearly.

In Exodus 19 the Israelites were referred to as the "house of Jacob," (v. 3) the "sons of Israel." You remember the story of Jacob. You remember his twin brother, Esau. You remember the backhanded theft of his brother's birthright, his go-round with Laban, his seven-year wait for the wrong wife, his overnight wrestling match with an angel at the Jabbok River.

Jacob. Or as he came to be called, Israel. For as the angel had said to him at sunrise, "Your name will no longer be Jacob. . . . It will be Israel because you have struggled with God and with men and have prevailed" (Gen. 32:28).

Up until this point these people standing before God at Sinai had only been known by their lineage. They were of the "house of Jacob." They were the "sons of Israel."

But at this defining moment in their history, we witness in some ways the birth of Israel as *God's people,* a new day in their relationship with him. John Durham writes, concerning this pivotal moment: "With the affirmative response, 'Israel,' a community of faith, transcending biological descendancy, could come into being."[1]

This covenant community would no longer be known just for where they had come from. They would now be known for who they were. They were the people of God, his own unique possession, designed to carry out a crucial role in reaching the nations, to fulfill God's kingdom purposes.

Even the seemingly out-of-the-way statement from the last part of Exodus 19:5 confirms this fact. When God said, "You will be My own possession out of all the peoples, *although all the earth is Mine,*" he was not simply affirming his ownership of the physical earth, his rightful claim as Creator. He was also using this phrase to describe his claim of Israel—not to give them privilege and standing alone but to give them purpose. They were to be his possession, not to be admired on a shelf but to be maneuvered full force into the world.

HIGHLY AND UNIQUELY PRIZED

Let's look a little deeper at what it means to be God's possession.

Some translations of the Bible render "my own possession" as being "my peculiar people," which comes from the Latin word meaning "property."[2] Perhaps all of us have known some "peculiar" fellow believers who resemble this translation. We are indeed a rather peculiar lot, aren't we? Yet with all of our peculiarities, God still calls us his own special treasure.

Some commentators have even linked this wording to an Akkadian term referring to a personal collection or hoard. The idea of a "peculiar" treasure, then—when seen in this light—is of a unique and exclusive possession among all the others.

God's people are like this to him—his crown jewel, his masterwork, his one of a kind.[3] And he never wanted Israel to forget it:

- "For you are a holy people belonging to the LORD your God. The LORD your God has chosen you to be His own possession out of all the peoples on the face of the earth" (Deut. 7:6, also 14:2).
- "And today the LORD has affirmed that you are His special people as He promised you, that you are to keep all His commands" (Deut. 26:18).
- "'They are Mine,' says the LORD of Hosts. 'a special possession on the day I am preparing. I will have compassion on them as a man has compassion on his son who serves him'" (Mal. 3:17).

These verses remind me of a loving dad who continually reminds his child how special and unique she is. He takes his child's face in his hands, looks deeply into her eyes, and affirms over and over that "you are my special child."

It boggles my mind to think that the sovereign God of the universe, the Creator of all that exists, has chosen to reach down from heaven, to take his children into his arms, and declare: "You are special to me." But this is the unquestionable reality of what the Bible teaches us. We are God's people by his own gracious choice. We are his most unique, most highly valuable possessions.

Yet while this truth is certainly glorious to behold, it comes with its share of responsibility . . . and its own adventurous reward!

People on the Move

People living in the ancient Near East, if they had any assets at all, possessed only two things of real value—land and jewelry. But the Hebrew word translated "possession" in Exodus 19:5 actually referred to property that could be *moved* and *relocated*—such as jewelry—as opposed to real estate, which could not be picked up and taken somewhere else.[4] Jewels, of course, were easily transportable and could be moved as the family traveled from one place to another.

This image of a *movable asset* meant that God could move his people as he desired in order to accomplish his set purpose.

What are the implications of this—of being God's movable possession? A few biblical examples come to mind:

Jeremiah. When God called him to be a prophet, Jeremiah considered himself unworthy of such a task. Listen to God's reply to Jeremiah's resistance: "Do not say, I am only a youth, for you will go wherever I send you and speak whatever I tell you. Do not be afraid of anyone, for I will be with you to deliver you" (Jer. 1:7–8). *Jeremiah was a movable possession.*

Joseph. You remember his story. His jealous brothers sold him as a slave, and he quickly found himself as a servant in Potiphar's house. From there he was thrown into an Egyptian jail, then transported upon his release into Pharaoh's court, where he became a ruler of Egypt. From this strategic, unexpected position, he was able to provide for his people's needs, rationing enough food to help them survive a seven-year bout of famine. And at some point, if not all along the way, God gave him the wisdom to see that he could use even the evil intent of his brothers to accomplish his own purposes. "It was not you who sent me here, but God," Joseph said to them. "He has made me a father to Pharaoh, lord of his entire household, and ruler over all the land of Egypt" (Gen. 45:8). *Joseph was a movable possession.*

Esther. When King Ahasuerus was looking for a queen, this orphaned Jewish girl—to everyone's surprise—found favor in his eyes. And when, through a case of political trickery and intrigue, the king sent out an edict to destroy the Jews, Esther was there to protect them, to stop the king's hand, to save the Israelites from annihilation. "Who knows," her uncle Mordecai had asked, "perhaps you have come to the kingdom for such a time as this" (Esther 4:14). *Esther was a movable possession.*

Philip. The Lord dispatched this evangelist from Samaria, where many were coming to Christ in response to his preaching, and sent him down to a road that descended from Jerusalem to Gaza. This was a "desert" road, the Bible tells us, not the kind of place where one would necessarily hang out—not the kind of place where Philip was likely to have the kind of success he was enjoying in Samaria. But he arrived just in time to meet an Ethiopian eunuch who was reading from the prophet Isaiah, and was able to "tell him the good news about Jesus, beginning from that Scripture" (Acts 8:35). The man was saved and baptized that very day. *Philip was a movable possession.*

I could go on. The Bible contains countless stories of how God placed his people in the exact place where he was working, at the exact time he needed them to be there. And we could add many other historical and modern-day and down-the-street-last-week stories to this endless list.

Then as now, as long as the earth endures, God will accomplish his kingdom purpose through the unique treasure of his covenant people—his prized and movable possessions.

How Movable Are You?

About twelve years ago God picked me up in Norfolk, Virginia, where I was pastoring an exciting and vibrant church, and set me down in Atlanta, Georgia, where I served our denomination as a church growth specialist. We built our dream house there and were planning to put down roots.

Then two years later God decided to move us to Texas, where I served as president of Southwestern Seminary in Fort Worth.

And now here I am, nine years later, sitting at my home office just north of Nashville, Tennessee, typing this manuscript. Looking back over the course of the last twelve years, God seems to have said to us, "You can build your dream home and make all the plans you want to make, but always remember that you are a movable treasure."

Perhaps, though, this illustration is a little too predictable. You're probably thinking, *Guys like you are supposed to do that, Ken. You're a preacher. Ministers are always being called to other assignments.*

Maybe so. But look back at the text of Exodus 19:5. It wasn't just Moses and the other leaders of Israel that God claimed as his movable possessions. He summoned the whole nation to this privileged calling. We are all—you, me, all of us—God's precious, movable possessions. God has a purpose for each one of us, wherever we are, wherever he places us.

This gives new meaning, then, to what we should be thinking about as we're standing in line at the supermarket, or waiting in the dentist's office, or shooting the breeze after a game of tennis. In any or all of these places—and countless others—God may have moved us there with a distinct purpose far beyond what we were expecting.

Perhaps, when stuck in line at the store, we can strike up a conversation with the person behind us, injecting a simple note of God's reality in the midst of a how-are-you-doing moment.

Perhaps we can spend a few minutes in the waiting room encouraging someone who's sitting near us rather than wasting our time reading last year's magazines.

Perhaps the growing friendship we're enjoying with our tennis partners will provide the necessary opportunity we need to tell them about Christ.

Who knows?

God has put us there anyway. And since he's done it on purpose, with deliberate intentionality, *shouldn't that make us wonder what kingdom agenda he has in mind?* If we know that God is always advancing his kingdom, and if we know that we are his movable resources, he can place us wherever he wants. He can use us wherever we are.

Starting today, ask God to make you sensitive to his activity as he moves you about in your community—as he puts into use one of his precious possessions.

Perhaps, though, this sounds a little too idealistic for your liking. You don't see your everyday life as being one big ministry opportunity after another. Instead, you simply have bills to pay and mouths to feed, so you head off into the day to do your work until quitting time. Perhaps you have children to watch or classes to attend, but not multitudes of lost people waiting to hear your testimony.

Please don't use this reality to discount your role as a "movable possession."

Some people truly misinterpret their responsibility as witnesses for Christ. They think, for example, that if they're talking to someone in the break room about their relationship with God or about some spiritual topic, they're exempted from being back at their post on time. They use their Christian witness as an excuse for slacking off on the job.

But not every ministry opportunity is a one-on-one conversation. In fact, God's movable possessions often declare the kingdom best by performing their work with excellence. They labor, not for the boss of the company, but for their King. Their work ethic demonstrates that everyday relevance of Christian living. It reveals an important aspect of their relationship with Christ.

So you may not feel like a priestly commodity while you're driving a truck or making a sale or crunching a number. But God has purposefully moved you into your position to model integrity and obedience, to exude joy in the midst of conflict, to seek solutions and harmony while others are griping and complaining and talking behind people's backs.

Nothing in our daily lives escapes either the responsibility or the privilege of kingdom living. Everything we do every day has the potential to show forth Christ's nature, to express the kingdom difference he's made in our lives.

So open up. And let God's Spirit move you.

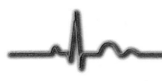

- In our society how do people generally react if a person or group of people is regarded as or treated like a possession?
- What evidence do you see that things are often valued more highly than people?
- Have you ever "treasured" a person? Have you ever been treasured?
- How do you feel about knowing that God treasures his people as his possessions?

Chapter 5

ENTRUSTED WITH GREATNESS

And you will be My kingdom of priests.

EXODUS 19:6

I ABSOLUTELY LOVE THE THEME of the previous chapter—the fact that we are a precious, yet movable treasure in the eyes of God. We are a possession that he not only embraces but also employs.

Perhaps you, too, had never really thought of yourself in this way. But now that we've seen this spelled out in Scripture, what do we take away from this understanding? What does it mean? What does a movable asset actually do?

The answer to this question begins to unfold in the nutrient-rich soil of Exodus 19:6, coinciding with the first mention of the word *kingdom* in the Bible as it relates to the people of God.

Throughout the earliest pages of the Old Testament, the stories of the patriarchs had hinted at the kingdom, implying its existence and foreshadowing its form. But here, in Exodus 19, God put his clear intentions into words, explaining to his chosen ones that they were to be a "kingdom of priests."

Bear in mind that there was no priestly class in Israel. We know from our own historical vantage point that the Levites would later become Israel's priestly tribe, and Aaron would later be appointed as high priest over the entire nation. But all of these happenings would come later. For now there was no precedent for this "kingdom of priests" in Israelite history. This was revolutionary. Unheard of. These people—all of them—had been chosen to take on the tasks of the priesthood. This was an awesome calling, a corporate calling, a unique calling.

It is our calling.

And just as the people of ancient Israel grappled with what all of this meant, we too join them in discovering some of the concrete realities that flow from this challenge. Among them are essentials like these:

Yahweh is King. A kingdom by definition must be ruled by a monarch. Unlike any other people on earth, the Israelites were to be ruled by the one true God of the universe. So are we.

They would be known by their relationship with him. Their identity, authority, and nobility would be wrapped up in their unique position with God, just as our identity in others' minds should first and foremost be the fact that we are Christians. Others should not think of us merely as musicians or soccer parents or natives of a certain home state or region of the country. Once they know us for any period of time at all, this one thing should be clear to them: more than anything we are servants of God.

Their role would be to extend the rule of the King. They were not only to meet the needs of their fellow countrymen but also to be used by God to advance his kingdom throughout the earth. The passion of God is for the nations to worship him. Israel had been redeemed and called for that purpose. As one writer has put it, they were to be a "kingdom run not by politicians depending upon strength and connivance, but by priests depending on faith in Yahweh, a servant nation instead of a ruling nation."[1] We too are to be actively seeking other people we can serve.

So we can summarize the practical aspects of this calling in just six words: *serve God and minister to others.*

It's that simple. And yet, of course, that difficult.

A CALL TO ALL

When we think of priests in our modern context, we think of the black shirt and the high collar. We think of those who are immediately recognized as being representatives of God and the religious ministry. Yet we may also think of priests as being detached from the everyday experiences of an ordinary person. We at least think of them as being set apart for a particular calling, distinct from the daily hammering and handwriting and homemaking of the average man or woman.

This is where the "kingdom of priests" differs from the norm.

This call of God for Israel to be a "kingdom of priests" extended to *everyone,* not just to a select few. They were *all* to be employed in these twin responsibilities: worshipping God and serving as a mediator between him and the other nations where he had sent them. Each one of them was to play an active part in extending the reign of the King on the earth by reaching the peoples *of* the earth. Walter Kaiser, in his book, *Mission in the Old Testament,* has articulated this purpose succinctly: "They were to be a nation for all times and for all peoples—distinctly marked and challenged to serve."[2]

Serving. This seems to be the heart of the priestly role.

That's why the "servant songs" of the Old Testament "uniquely embody the 'kingdom of priests' motif, and afford a transition to the New Testament doctrines of the high priesthood of Jesus and the priesthood of all Christians."[3] Through these poetic prophecies, Isaiah challenged Israel to assume the priestly role they were called to embody. We, too, can learn from what they say:

"The Spirit of the Lord GOD is on Me, because the LORD has anointed Me to bring good news to the poor. He has sent Me to heal the brokenhearted, to proclaim liberty to the captives, and freedom to the prisoners" (Isa. 61:1). Jesus, you remember, read from this text at the synagogue in Nazareth and declared that "this Scripture has been fulfilled in your hearing" (Luke 4:21). And so, as Christ's followers, these same ministries remain our priestly calling: to share the good news of salvation, to minister to the hurting, to make God's love real to the world.

The prophet seems to be speaking to Israel when he reminds them, "You will be called the LORD's priests; they will speak of you as ministers of God" (Isa. 61:6). Isaiah emphasized the role they should play *and* the name they should be known by.

It is important to notice, however, that the priestly role of the suffering servant transcends the nation of Israel: "It is not enough for you to be My servant raising up the tribes of Jacob and restoring the protected ones of Israel. I will also make you a light for the nations, to be My salvation to the ends of the earth" (Isa. 49:6).

To be God's priests is a calling for all of us, a calling for us to serve all people.

In many ways this is the essence of kingdom living: *to serve other people in Jesus' name.* Not all of us are in a position to be great soul winners and evangelists (although more than we probably think). But in *building relationships with other people*—the ones who are right next door, right across the hall, right in the flow of our daily lives—we serve as a window for them to see and feel and experience God's love and grace. In serving other people—in any number of countless ways God can reveal to us—we make investments in the kingdom.

We serve as his "kingdom of priests."

Living Stones, Living Sacrifices

Exodus 19 became the basis for the New Testament doctrine of what we call the "priesthood of all believers," the idea that Christians are able to have direct access to God through Christ alone, without requiring a human go-between. We find this concept most clearly articulated in 1 Peter 2:5: "You yourselves, as living stones, are being built up into a spiritual house for a *holy priesthood,* to offer spiritual sacrifices acceptable to God through Jesus Christ."

Notice, too, how this imagery of "living stones" makes an undeniable connection between this verse and Exodus 19:5–6, the priestly passage where we are said to be God's precious "possession." We—the people of God, his prized and movable treasures—are the "living stones" the King is using to build up his house and advance his kingdom on earth.

My wife made an interesting observation about the challenge God has brought upon himself by choosing to build with "living stones" as opposed to inanimate ones. Living stones have a mind or will of their own. They can often be obstinate and hard to work with, insistent on wanting things done their way. Wouldn't it be much easier for him to accomplish his work by using less *lively stones*?

But one of the duties of the priest, you remember, was to bring sacrifices before the Lord. And because we are "living stones," we are able to bring him "living sacrifices"—the only offerings which are "acceptable" in his sight.

I find this especially encouraging. Have you ever thought you had nothing worth offering to God? This is a tragic lie that can keep us from fulfilling our priestly role. First Peter 2:5 makes clear that our sacrifices are acceptable to God, not because of how they stack up against all the others but simply because they are offered to God through Jesus Christ. Our great High Priest presents our "living sacrifices" himself to the Father. This is all that's required to make our gifts "acceptable."

But what kinds of "living sacrifices" does a kingdom person make to God?

Our bodies. "Therefore, brothers, by the mercies of God, I urge you to present your bodies as a living sacrifice, holy and pleasing to God; this is your spiritual worship" (Rom. 12:1). By continuing to read though Romans 12, we discover that Paul is not only talking about the purity of our *personal* bodies but also the united sacrifices made by the body of believers, the church. By offering back to him all the physical abilities and spiritual gifts he has given to us—as individuals and as churches—we fulfill a major part of our priestly duties.

Our worship. "Therefore, through Him let us continually offer up to God a sacrifice of praise, that is, the fruit of our lips that confess His name" (Heb. 13:15). Have you ever thought about worship as being a priestly sacrifice you can offer to God? This perspective should arrest our attention the next time we approach worship lackadaisically, halfheartedly focusing on God as the object of our praise and adoration.

Our service. "Don't neglect to do good and to share, for God is pleased with such sacrifices" (Heb. 13:16). By actively planning to be thoughtful, watchful, caring, and compassionate, we meet the needs of those around us and please our Father at the same time.

Our witness. Paul talked about being a "priest of God's good news," with his stated purpose being that "the offering of the Gentiles may be acceptable" as a result of receiving God's salvation (Rom. 15:16). He saw his sharing of the gospel message as a stewardship, an act of priestly service and obedience, a way to help others experience the joy of Christ's presence and acceptance.

PRIVILEGE OR PASSION?

When we started this chapter, we saw that Israel had been chosen by God to be entrusted with this priestly privilege.

Chosen. This word has a wonderful ring to it. We love to be chosen. Can you remember those anxious moments when you stood on the playground, wondering if the captains would select you when they were choosing up sides for softball? Perhaps you can remember what it was like to be selected to sing a solo part in the Christmas musical, to stand there waiting for the names to be announced, and to hear . . . yours.

It makes us feel special to be chosen.

But when *chosen* is interpreted only in terms of special privilege, it can create a sense of arrogance and be offensive to others.

We are all too quickly reminded of the teacher's pet, the child who was given special privileges not accessible by the average student. Israel faced this timeless temptation, the selfish appeal to interpret their uniqueness in terms of privilege and not responsibility.

Tragically Israel failed to take advantage of the opportunity to be a royal priesthood, to extend God's rule to all the nations. They instead developed spiritual myopia, viewing their calling only in terms of privilege and not in terms of their noble mission to the nations.

But the privilege and task that Israel rejected was not nullified. We find its ultimate fulfillment in the pages of the New Testament. Jesus, the great High Priest, modeled this role of reaching the nations, offering himself as the atoning sacrifice, paving the way for a new priestly community to be made up of believers in Christ.

Israel's calling is now ours. We have been redeemed through the blood of Christ and entrusted with the greatness of his saving message and godly character.

The question for us, his "kingdom of priests," is this: will we deem it worth the sacrifice?

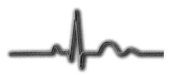

- How can someone be both great and a servant? Can you think of someone in your life who has had both of these attributes?
- How does the concept of sacrificial living fit in our world today?
- How can people today become "living sacrifices"?

A King
and His Purpose

Chapter 6

SEE THE DIFFERENCE?

And you will be . . . My holy nation.

EXODUS 19:6

HAVE YOU EVER HAD a vivid memory of some seemingly insignificant childhood event? For example, I can still remember window-shopping as a kid. Perhaps the reason I enjoyed it so much—and remember it so clearly—is because our family had such meager resources, we knew that *looking* was about as close as we were ever going to get to buying the larger items in the window.

Actually, my earliest memory of window-shopping involved, not real windows, but the Sears and Roebuck catalog. When it arrived at our house every year before Christmas, I would rifle straight to the toy section, where I would longingly gaze at the items showcased there. In fact, I would often dog-ear some of the pages in hopes that one of my parents might notice.

I also recall window-shopping as a boy along the streets of downtown Thomasville, North Carolina. I remember wondering, as I would go from one store to the next, *How did the owner of this particular store know how to put the exact objects I wanted in their window?* This question really puzzled me as a child. Of course,

I know now that the storekeepers didn't *really* know what I wanted. They simply used the showcase to create the desire. Their well-lit, intricately planned window was designed to whet my appetite for the showcased products.

Yes, you can really do a lot with a good store window.

That's why many, many years ago, God set up a store window of sorts at the base of Mount Sinai. Through a rather insignificant tribe of people, not chosen through any merit of their own, God established a nation through which he could showcase his own greatness. They weren't to be known for their slick advertising or fancy slogans. They were simply to be known for the God whose glory shone through their front window—a window designed to be thrown open to the world so that people might walk by and look in and wonder and worship.

This was God's purpose for his people, Israel. This was one of his key reasons for making them "a holy nation."

SETTING UP SHOP

This word *holy* means "set apart." It's unfortunate, though, that we sometimes distinguish between the synonyms *holy* and *wholly.* In truth, Israel had been set apart—made *holy*—so that they would belong *wholly* to God. As God's possession, their national objective was to bring him pleasure and serve his purposes—to be wholly his.

Does this sound selfish to you on God's part? It shouldn't. What greater significance could Israel have than to showcase the One who was solely responsible for making them who they were—a kingdom of priests, a prized possession, a nation set apart by their relationship with the one true God?

Likewise, what greater significance can *we* have than to show-case the God who has saved us?

This shouldn't strike us as being demeaning to ourselves or presumptuous of God. He has made clear in Scripture that we are of the highest value to him. Rather than threatening our self-esteem, showcasing him should be the ultimate expression of our worth. Yes, we may be merely a window, but we are his *chosen* win-dow—a window to the most extraordinary treasure there is.

When we were welcomed by grace into his kingdom, set apart for his eternal purposes, this meant that our time, our resources, and our schedule were no longer ours to control. Our lives were placed at the disposal of our Redeemer.

This unique, "set apart" status is what gives us our uncommon freedom in Christ. When God moves us in accordance with his own eternal plans, he fills our lives with unexpected yet purpose-filled opportunity. When we serve the desires of the One who cre-ated and redeemed us, we can be assured that he keeps our best interests at heart because he loves us and has chosen us as his own.

God had chosen Israel in this way not because they had any special uniqueness as a nation but in order for them to be a showcase of his blessing. He wanted to demonstrate to the world what living in a covenant relationship with him could produce in people's lives. The blessings he promised to bestow upon his chosen people were *never* intended to glorify Israel but to show-case his own goodness so that all the nations of the earth would be drawn to *him* through *them*.

My mind leaps ahead to the pages of the New Testament, to God's new covenant community. I think of Paul, who saw himself as the chief of sinners, chosen by God as an example of someone through whom "Christ Jesus might demonstrate the utmost patience as an example to those who would believe in Him for eternal life" (1 Tim. 1:16). Paul, this persecutor turned believer, was not saved merely to receive God's blessing. He was also saved to serve as a showcase of God's perfect patience.

Have you ever asked yourself why God saved you? There is more than one answer to this question, of course. But did God redeem you just to assure you a heavenly home? Or did he perhaps have more than one great purpose in mind?

I believe so. By virtue of your redemption and calling, God has fashioned you into a shiny new window for his showcase. Through you he has chosen to demonstrate to the world the blessings of living in relationship with him. Through you he desires to gather glory for himself and draw others into his kingdom.

His blessings are given to be conveyed, not consumed.

This is what it means to be *wholly* his.

ALL THE DIFFERENCE IN THE WORLD

Being holy, of course, means more than that. While the primary meaning of *holy* is to be "set apart" in terms of service, we can readily see why it must also mean *holy* in behavior and lifestyle. The God we serve is himself holy. And if we are to be his showcase window to the world, we must reflect his holiness.

Ours is a world where we are often lured into being near carbon copies of our culture—Christian up to a point yet cool enough to know when we're taking it too far. We are rewarded with the world's acceptance when our tastes and standards look more like the prevailing norms and less like the prescribed Word of God. We feel a little more comfortable when we fit in.

But our calling as a "holy nation" is a calling to be different.

It is critically important that we come to terms with this. Kingdom people are promised the most rewarding, fulfilling, satisfying life on earth. But it comes at the cost of being willing to be different. It means we must conform to the character of the One who calls us.

This is worth taking seriously.

God did. After Israel's long experience of wandering in the wilderness as a result of disobedience, he reminded a new generation that his calling for them had not changed. "For you are a holy people belonging to the LORD your God. The LORD has chosen you to be His special people out of all the peoples on the face of the earth" (Deut. 14:2).

Throughout the remainder of Deuteronomy 14, he spoke of holiness in terms of dietary regulations and the giving of tithes. While we understand that many of the ceremonial laws of the Old Testament no longer apply to the new covenant in Christ, this passage still teaches us an important principle. Our lifestyle decisions, including issues as practical as our health and our money management, are all to reflect the character of the God we serve.

Sound overwhelming? It would be—except that God has promised to achieve this holiness himself . . . *through us.* Our job as believers—as kingdom people—is not so much to *commit* ourselves to God as it is to *submit* ourselves to him.

Notice the progression in Leviticus 20:7–8: "Consecrate yourselves and be holy, for I am the LORD your God. Keep My statutes and do them; I am the LORD who sets you apart," who makes you holy. As free moral agents who had chosen to enter into a covenant relationship with God, the people were to give themselves *wholly* to the task of *holiness,* to "consecrate" themselves. But through their yieldedness and obedience, God promised to set them apart, to sanctify them—to make them holy. Our holiness is his job.

This phrase "the LORD who sets you apart" or "the LORD who sanctifies you" is one of God's many names found in the Old Testament—Jehovah Mekadesh. This is who he is—the One who makes us holy.[1] Holiness, then—like the fruit of the Spirit—is a quality of life that can only be produced by God.

This should take some pressure off of us. It's not that he's giving us permission to be lazy about our behaviors and attitudes. He's simply giving us permission to be free, to let him do through us what only he can do anyway.

Being holy, being different from the landscape, being a living example of God's character, is truly the work of the Holy Spirit in our lives. There's no way to formulate it, no way to adequately describe exactly how it happens. But as we give ourselves to the Lord and his kingdom, he transforms us day by day into clearer windows—the better to see him.

THE OBEDIENCE HABIT

Israel had been redeemed and was preparing both to inhabit the promised land and to reach the nations. So how were they to live? Once they had settled their families in this land inhabited by pagan nations, how were they to maintain their distinctive qualities as a people related to God?

This question is as relevant today as it was thousands of years ago. We, too, are inhabitants of a largely pagan culture. We live in our world with the kingdom purpose of serving those around us and letting Christ's glory shine through our lives.

But how do we really do that?

Many writers have approached this topic of holiness over the years, offering us numerous suggestions on how we can achieve such purity of heart and soul. Some people read these books looking for a simple formula, hoping to find a low-commitment path to holiness.

It's kind of like dieting. The experts lead us from fad to fad, creating as many side effects as they do success stories. But it basically boils down to this: to lose weight, we eat less and we exercise more. It's a fairly simple formula.

So for those who are looking for the seven simple steps to holiness, I'll give you just one: we experience holiness by being obedient to the Lord. This is because:

- Partial obedience is *total* disobedience.
- Delayed obedience is *present tense* disobedience.
- Thus, full obedience is the only *cure* for disobedience.

I know that many people today—many Christians, in fact—do not live consistently by the teachings of God's Word. Truth is, we all face a daily struggle to let his truth capture our affections and control our behavior. But obedience is the only proper response for a kingdom person.

1. *We obey because he's redeemed us.* "For the grace of God has appeared, with salvation for all people, instructing us to deny godlessness and worldly lusts and to live in a sensible, righteous, and godly way in the present age" (Titus 2:11–12).

2. *We obey because he is holy.* "As the One who called you is holy, you also are to be holy in all your conduct; for it is written, 'Be holy, because I am holy'" (1 Pet. 1:15–16).

3. *We obey because this is his purpose for us.* "Look, today I set before you a blessing and a curse: there will be a blessing, if you obey the commands of the LORD your God I am giving you today" (Deut. 11:26–27). Obedience opens the floodgate for blessing, which enables us to be a blessing to others.

ON THE HEM OF HOLINESS

I recently came across a passage of Scripture that, if I'd ever noticed it before, I honestly don't remember it. I have since shared it with others through sermons and conversations, and I almost always hear someone tell me, "I've never heard that verse before."

But I believe the Holy Spirit has led me to this Scripture for a reason: to teach me that the purpose of our everyday pursuit of holiness is not simply to experience victory for ourselves. We are not to obey God in the hopes of securing and storing up his blessing. We are not called to be "a holy nation" so that we can look down our pious noses as the world trips over its own half-truths.

One of God's kingdom desires in making us holy is to showcase his mercy, to draw sinful men and women to himself.

Here's how the prophet Zechariah described it:

"'Many peoples and strong nations will come to seek the LORD of Hosts in Jerusalem and to plead for the LORD's favor.' The LORD of Hosts says this: 'In those days, 10 men from nations of every language will grab the robe of a Jewish man tightly, urging,

"Let us go with you, for we have heard that God is with you"'"
(Zech. 8:22–23).

Israel was to be the recipient of God's blessing not because of any inherent merit on their part but because God desired that his covenant community reflect his glory among the nations. He put them in his showcase and cast his light upon them so that they could reflect his glory, so that others would tug on their arms and say, "Let us go with you, for we have heard that God is with you."

Today this calling is ours—to be a "holy nation" of believers in Christ, to live in such a way that others can see the difference . . . and want our Deliverer.

Hear the prophet Isaiah speak this living truth into your heart: "Arise, shine, for your light has come, and the glory of the LORD shines over you. For look, darkness covers the earth, and total darkness the peoples; but the LORD will shine over you, and His glory will appear over you. Nations will come to your light, and kings to the brightness of your radiance" (Isa. 60:1–3).

So polish the glass. Purify each pane. Scrub away every blemish, any desire you may have for people to pay more attention to you than the One you were created to showcase.

The Lord of glory wants to shine through your front window.

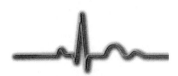 *A recent survey conducted by the Barna Research Group reported that 65 percent of Americans are concerned about the future, with roughly 74 percent of those citing moral decay in America and the world as their primary concern.* (Source: Baptist Press)

- Do you feel "set apart" or that you are "wandering in the wilderness"? Why?
- What is the cost of being "holy" today?
- If our nation were holy, what would be different?
- If you were holy, how would your life change?

Chapter 7

KNOWN BY HIS NAME

And who is like Your people Israel? God came to one nation on earth in order to redeem a people for Himself, to make a name for Himself, and to perform for them great and awesome acts, driving out nations and their gods before Your people You redeemed for Yourself from Egypt.

2 SAMUEL 7:23

WE HAVE ALL READ numerous stories of individuals who set out to make a name for themselves. Perhaps it was a young athlete from a poor family who used his athletic prowess to rise to the top of his sport. We love to read about entrepreneurs who, through tireless skill and tenacity, have conquered the marketplace with their products.

But in the end, no matter how much fame and success flow from this kind of household name recognition, the payoff is never as satisfying as they thought it would be. The headaches and hassles that come along with celebrity are oftentimes not worth the acclaim and attention these people receive.

So in many of the most important ways, those who set out in life to make a name for themselves get a lot less than they hoped for.

But when God chose to make a name for *himself* through his covenant people, he freely gave us everything we could want. And those of us who willingly embody the name of Christ in our lives, who seek to be known by our nearness and relationship to him, will enjoy a life that can never be found by those who seek a name for themselves.

If we don't know this from experience, we can see it in a man who discovered this truth in a place where there's usually only room for one king. Truly, in King David's palace, only one name belonged on the front door.

BUILDING PLANS

God declared his plan to give Israel an earthly king as early as Deuteronomy 17: "When you enter the land the LORD your God is giving you, take possession of it, live in it, and say, 'We want to appoint a king over us like all the nations around us,' you are to appoint over you the king the LORD your God chooses" (vv. 14–15a). This king would not rule like typical earthly kings, the ones of the other nations, the ones Israel had seen and heard about. The king of Israel would not depend on military might (v. 16), or use his position for personal gain (v. 17), but would obey God's law and fear him (v. 19).

In other words, this king would work to establish *God's* kingdom, not his own.

David, of course, became the greatest of these kings many hundreds of years later. And after he had begun to rule, after he had built a cedar house for himself and was living in peace, his heart was moved to do something great—to build a house for God.

But why?

To understand this passion, we need to look back at Deuteronomy 12 and familiarize ourselves with the instructions God had given the people of Israel just before they entered the promised land. The Lord told them:

1. *They were to obey God's law.* For as long as they lived in the land, they were to "be careful to follow" everything God had told them to do (v. 1).

2. *They were to destroy the places of pagan worship.* "Tear down . . . smash . . . burn up . . . cut down . . . wipe out their names from every place" (vv. 2–3). God couldn't have been any clearer about this. These are some serious action verbs.

3. *They were to build a house of worship.* God said he would show them the place to build when they got there. He would tell them when the time was right. But one thing was already for sure: this house would be a place "to put His name" (v. 5).

And David wanted to be the one who would see this promise kept . . . in stone and marble and gold and glory.

At first the prophet Nathan responded approvingly to David's noble plan, not seeing any reason this wouldn't be a great idea (2 Sam. 7:3). But during the night God gave Nathan a different directive: Yes, a king would indeed build a house of worship for Israel—"a house for My name," the Lord said. But it wouldn't be David who would build it. This privilege would pass instead to David's son, Solomon.

How would David react to such news? Anger? Depression? Would he send out an appeal anyway for laborers and building materials, proceeding with his plans whether God wanted a house of worship built for him or not?

No, David was nearly speechless. The Bible says he swallowed everything Nathan had said, then went in and "sat in the LORD's presence" (v. 18a).

You can almost hear him even now, whispering in low tones: "Who am I, Lord GOD, and what is my house that You have brought me this far?" (v. 18b)—from shepherding his daddy's sheep to shepherding God's people. "What more can David say to You?" (v. 20).

Certainly, he was disappointed to see the building of the temple pass him by. Yet he knew in his heart that this undertaking wasn't really about him or his kingdom.

This was about *God* and *his* kingdom.

And God was prepared to honor this kind of humility in David. For even in delaying the privilege of temple-building a generation, God promised that he would "establish the throne of [David's] kingdom forever" (v. 13).

What more could a kingdom person ask?

That's why David could react to this setback with song. That's why instead of moaning and complaining that he would be long dead before God's temple was completed, he could break forth in praise: "You are great, Lord GOD. There is no one like You, and there is no God besides You" (v. 22a).

Yes, the news Nathan had brought him was hard to take. But when a person's only concern is the kingdom, when a person has a true vision of the greatness of God, when a person is willing to invest himself in something bigger than his own lifetime, his whole perspective on life changes.

It works the same way with us. As long as God's name is exalted, a kingdom person can be OK with anything.

ONE BIG, HAPPY KINGDOM

David understood this. He knew it wasn't one man but one whole nation—from one generation to another over time—which God had established to embody his name on the earth. And so David could find freedom in releasing his plans to this reality, to the higher purposes of God's kingdom.

As we've been seeing throughout Israel's history, God was looking for a people who would embrace his mission, embody his name, and obey his Word. Their entire lifestyle was to be regulated in order to give a clear earthly witness to his name and character. They were to stand out among the nations, not to make a name for themselves but to make a name for their God and King.

"Who is like Your people Israel?" David asked. "God came to one nation on earth in order to redeem a people for Himself, to make a name for Himself, and to perform for them great and awesome acts, driving out nations and their gods before Your people You redeemed for Yourself from Egypt" (v. 23).

There was nothing all that special about this one nation. Other nations, in fact, were more numerous and powerful. But God had redeemed Israel from Pharaoh's whip and workhouse, not merely to show them mercy but to "make a name for Himself." Their covenant relationship with Yahweh distinguished them from all other people in the world.

The importance and significance of this fact had never been lost on David, who prayed that God would do what he had promised concerning the temple and the kingly line, "so that Your name will be exalted forever, when it is said, 'The LORD of Hosts is God over Israel'" (v. 26).

God's kingdom, embodying God's name, is all that matters.

Surely this is what the psalmist meant when he sang, "Not to us, LORD, not to us, but to Your name give glory because of Your faithful love, because of Your truth. Why should the nations say, 'Where is their God?'" (Ps. 115:1).

Yes, there is joy and strength and lasting purpose in embodying the name of the Lord.

FOR HIS NAME'S SAKE

Let's look at this name of God a little more closely.

God's name stands for his character. He revealed his name, in its many different forms and aspects, as a way of inviting his people to live with him in a dynamic, intimate relationship.

Samuel clearly understood the relational nature of God's name when he encouraged Israel as they prepared to engage the Philistines in battle: "The LORD will not abandon His people, *because of His great name* and because He has determined to make you His own people" (1 Sam. 12:22).

After the defeat at Ai, Joshua tore his clothes and fell down before the Lord, crying out: "When the Canaanites and all who live in the land hear about this, they will surround us and wipe out our name from the earth. Then what will You do about *Your great name*?" (Josh. 7:9). Joshua understood that the defeat of Israel impacted not just the reputation of the nation but the name of the Lord. He called on God to act for his name's sake.

This is God's way. To act "for his name's sake"—to act in a manner consistent with his nature and character—is something he declares many times throughout the Bible. When he leads us in paths of righteousness (Ps. 23:3), forgives our sins (Ps. 25:11), guides us through the snares and seductions of life (Ps. 31:3), delivers us from our sins (Ps. 79:9), deals kindly with us (Ps. 109:21), and, indeed, lets us live at all (Ps. 143:11), he does these things "for His name's sake."

We exist as God's people, alive and thriving in God's kingdom, to embody his name. Pure and simple.

ONE NAME, ONE KINGDOM, FOREVER

This name we bear is the only name that will last forever.

That's why we cannot leave a chapter like this without a quick, final glimpse at the promise of an eternal kingdom. When the Lord told David that he would establish the work of Solomon's hands in building the temple, he went on to say that he would "appoint him over My house and My kingdom forever, and his throne will be established forever" (1 Chron. 17:14).

J. A. Thompson, commenting on this passage, notes: "God is the real King of Israel, and the kingdom is his. . . . In the oracle of Nathan, there is a messianic significance that can hardly be over-estimated."[1] We know now that the Lord's reference to "forever" in his message to David found its ultimate fulfillment in Jesus, the *Son* of David . . . who was born in Bethlehem, the *city* of David . . . and who lives forever on the throne of his Father's kingdom. We, too, will live with him forever.

Still, we may long to see in our eighty years or so the fulfillment of all the things God has started in us. But neither we nor God's kingdom is limited to a human lifetime. Because we will tread on streets of gold and live forever in the glory of God's eternal kingdom, we can live free from the restraints of now and next week.

Yes, those of us who embody his name today can already enjoy a taste of his eternal kingdom. We live and serve and work and play in a kingdom that has no boundaries, no restrictions, no limits, and no end. This joyful task of embodying God's name places us squarely in the middle of God's will for this hour and forever in the freedom of his purposes for eternity.

So when someone asks you, "How can you be nice to that guy after he's been so ugly to you?" or, "How are you able to be so patient with your children?" or, "Why does your family seem so happy and connected?" tell them there's a name for what they see in you.

His name is Jesus.

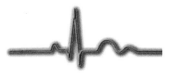

- How well does the church today, God's house, represent his name?

- If all your friends knew of God was what they had learned from you, if you are a Christian, what would they know of God and his name?

Chapter 8

HOW A HOUSE
BECOMES A HOME

**Even for the foreigner who is not of Your people Israel
but has come from a distant land because of Your name.**

1 KINGS 8:41

CAN YOU REMEMBER the mounting anticipation and excitement you experienced as a child when Christmas approached?

Oh, how the weeks, days, and finally even the last remaining hours seemed to creep along. By Christmas Eve you had searched in all the typical hiding places to see if the gifts you'd requested were going to appear on that glorious morning. Then the day finally dawned! You rushed down the stairs to celebrate this long-awaited day of fulfillment—to claim the promises, as well as the surprises, of Christmas.

No doubt the nation of Israel must have awakened on the day of the temple dedication with even more intense feelings than these. Many had watched the massive temple being slowly constructed, stone upon stone. The arduous, exacting task had created in the onlookers a feverish sense of expectation, and the delay of the dedication to make it coincide with the Feast of Tabernacles had only heightened their breathlessness.

The stage had been set.

On this great day of unprecedented pageantry and drama, Solomon assembled the people in order—the elders, the heads of the tribes, and the leaders of the Israelite households. Then the priests layered themselves into position, carrying into the temple the ark of the covenant—the movable symbol of God's presence—as well as all the implements of worship.

I don't believe our casual culture can begin to imagine the sheer exuberance the Israelites must have felt as they observed this solemn yet triumphal procession—the ark being brought to its rightful place, housed in the beautiful building where God had promised his name would dwell. About as close as we can come to measuring the mood of the celebration is from this graphic hint: 1 Kings 8:5 tells us that King Solomon and the congregation of Israel had sacrificed so many sheep and oxen in the flurry of worship leading up to this event, the people in charge of keeping count of the carcasses had given up even trying!

Then—as the ark was being placed in the temple, a cloud representing the presence of God filled the house of the Lord. His awesome presence was so overwhelming, the priests could not even continue to minister, "for the glory of the LORD filled the temple" (v. 11). Solomon, taken aback at the glory of the moment, cried out in triumph to God: "The LORD said that He would dwell in thick darkness, but I have indeed built an exalted temple for You, a place for Your dwelling forever" (vv. 12–13).

This was simply too much to keep to themselves.

WELCOME, STRANGER

We have touched on this idea throughout the book, but perhaps this moment in Israel's history provides the clearest, most compelling example of God's kingdom purposes for his people. The blessing of the temple was indeed an extraordinary opportunity for worship—a rousing, incomparable display of raw wonder and reverence. The people probably never felt so connected to their forefathers—the ones who had seen God pound the Egyptians with hail and darkness and frogs in their beds, who had watched as the Red Sea peeled its waters off the ocean bed and paved a course to freedom and deliverance.

Here he was again—this God who had led their families by flame and cloud through the wilderness—hovering low enough now for them almost to feel the spray of his glory. What could the people do but bow and weep and lift their hands in praise?

We were made for this.

Kingdom people cannot survive without worship.

But the blessing of the temple cannot be completely understood without seeing that this building was designed for more than Israel's worship needs, that it possessed an even broader purpose. In fact, *every blessing bestowed by God on his people*—including this house of prayer and worship—*is intended to have a global, eternal impact.*

When Solomon prayed the following words at the temple dedication ceremony, he was leaving us a charge that still rings in our ears this many centuries hence: "Even for the foreigner who is not of Your people Israel but has come from a distant land because of Your name—for they will hear of Your great name, mighty hand, and outstretched arm, and will come and pray toward this temple—may You hear in heaven, Your dwelling place, and do according to all the foreigner asks You for. Then all the people on earth will know Your name, to fear You as Your people Israel do and know that this temple I have built is called by Your name" (1 Kings 8:41–43).

The modern-day parallels, which this passage brings to mind, are too great for me to pass up. When we have a desire to build a new church building or to add to our existing structure, do we plan and build with the "foreigner" in mind? Naturally, this doesn't mean that our churches should be designed for wooing visitors at the expense of worshipping God. But because drawing the outsider is one of God's specified purposes for the house where his name dwells, should we not ask the question, "What impact will this new facility have on our ability to reach the unsaved? Are our plans for this expansion the highest and best use of God's resources as he implements his kingdom plans through us?"

CALLING ALL COMERS

This desire for the foreigner to enjoy God's blessings may have been a "foreign" thought to many in Israel, but it was always at the heart of God's purposes for them.

David had expressed God's passion for others in this way: "All the nations You have made will come and bow down before You, LORD, and will honor Your name. For You are great and perform wonders; You alone are God" (Ps. 86:9–10).

In the verses leading up to these, David had boldly prayed for his own needs, assured that the Lord would answer him. Yet because he understood the heart of this prayer-answering God of Israel, he was equally certain that many people of other nations would also come to the Lord and find him to be exactly who David had found him to be: the one and only, wonder-working God.

The prophet Isaiah also pictured this reality—the nations running to Israel because God had sought them out and had been seen in his people. Speaking to Israel, he says: "You will summon a nation you do not know, and nations who do not know you will run to you. For the LORD your God, even the Holy One of Israel, has glorified you" (Isa. 55:5).

This image of nations running to the people of God is almost too wonderful to imagine. It's as though we're a flower garden, and all who pass by wonder how these blooms contain such fire and color. "For as the earth brings forth its growth, and as a garden enables what is sown to spring up, so the Lord GOD will cause righteousness and praise to spring up before all the nations" (Isa. 61:11).

A garden sprout doesn't put forth any willful effort of its own in order to spring from the ground. God has simply designed it for this purpose. In the same way, God's people have been designed to display his righteousness and praise, causing our Christian witness naturally to spring up from us.

This is God's heart. This is God's purpose for his kingdom people. God has placed in us his name, his nature, and his character. And his name looks best on us not only when we're worshipping him in our Christian circles but also when we're shining our light for those who wouldn't necessarily come looking for him on their own.

GOD IN US, NOT IN IT

Some commentators miss the point of this section, I think. They suggest that the splendor of the temple itself would draw the foreigner in God's direction. No doubt, some of the Israelites may have shared this idea.

But Solomon's prayer at the temple dedication captured the true intent of God's vision, that the foreigner "will hear of [His] great name, mighty hand, and outstretched arm, and will come and pray toward this temple" (1 Kings 8:42). God's name was the initial draw; the temple was merely the destination. God's house was to be a place for his name to dwell, but God's people were to be a nation who dwelled in his name—everywhere they went.

Perhaps we are tempted to think the same thing when we build our magnificent churches, or when we worship to the beat of a certain kind of music, or when we preach in a particularly engaging style. All of these things are fine in themselves, and God uses them to perform his work and speak to people's hearts. But nothing is more effective in touching people's lives than the daily witness and example of one kingdom person. We who embody his name are his magnets to the world.

It has always been this way. The temple—in all its glory—was still only a physical reminder of all the things God had done for his people. God imprinted his name on Israel's hearts, and he stretched out his hand of blessing to them. The foreigner will "run to you," Isaiah said, not because your church has a sharp youth ministry but because the Lord has "glorified you"—his kingdom people.

The Lord gives us an example of this—the drawing power of his name imprinted on the life of a person—in the story of the Queen of Sheba, very soon after the temple dedication. She traveled fifteen hundred miles from the Persian Gulf region to Jerusalem, her camel caravan loaded down with spices and precious gifts, because she had heard of the wisdom of Solomon.

But she had come for more than that! "The queen of Sheba heard about Solomon's fame connected with *the name of the LORD* and came to test him with difficult questions" (1 Kings 10:1).

The temple was impressive, I'm sure. Solomon's splendor was immense. But the thing that turned the head of this wealthy queen was the indelible stamp of God on one of his people's lives. That's why, after sufficiently picking his brain, she concluded that the rumors she had heard about Solomon's brilliance didn't really tell half the story. This pagan queen recognized God's blessing in Solomon's life, saying, "He delighted in you and put you on the throne of Israel, because of the LORD's eternal love for Israel. He has made you king to carry out justice and righteousness" (v. 9).

God's name was visible in his people, even from a distance.

And so we continue to see throughout the Scripture the weaving together of three threads:

1. God called a people to *embrace his mission*—to be his chosen instruments in drawing the nations to himself.
2. He established a covenant relationship with them so they would *embody his name* and represent his nature and character to the world.
3. And he commanded that they *obey his Word,* producing a brand of holiness that demonstrated to all the noticeable difference he made in their lives.

This is still the way—the only way—our houses of worship become a home for those who are tired of slogging through a world of senseless sin and recurring disappointments.

And it's how this "temple" we live in every moment of our lives—this human body redeemed and renewed by the blood of

Christ—helps the people within our reach find a home in the warm embrace of God, wherever he places us throughout the day.

So make sure you keep his name on the door and his light in the window. There's always someone out there who's looking for home.

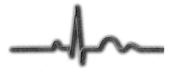

- When have you felt exuberant joy? How did that joy relate to the name of God?
- Do you have confidence in the integrity of God's promises today? Why/Why not?
- What is needed for revival in our country? For personal revival?
- Who are "the foreigners" in your life who need to know about God and find welcome in his house?

Chapter 9

WHEN GOD'S PEOPLE QUIT CARING

When they came to the nations where they went, they profaned My holy name, because it was said about them: These are the people of the LORD, yet they had to leave His land in exile.

EZEKIEL 36:20

WE ASSOCIATE PARTICULAR NAMES with certain events or characteristics. When we hear the name Lee Harvey Oswald, for example, we immediately think of November 22, 1963—the assassination of President Kennedy. When we hear the name Hitler or Stalin, we think of the worst forms of hatred and abusive power, the cruel extermination of large numbers of people. The same can be true of entire nations or people groups. What kinds of images come to mind, say, when we think of the Vikings?

Names stand for something. For good or evil.

God had chosen Israel from among all the nations of the earth to be his showcase people, redeeming them in order to make a name for himself, blessing them in order that others would see their righteousness and be drawn to their God. They were to be "a glorious crown in the LORD's hand, and a royal diadem" in his palm (Isa. 62:3).

But they became, instead, a slap in God's face. This nation, so uniquely blessed by almighty God, failed to live up to its divine potential. Rather than *exalting* his name among the nations, their actions *profaned* his name in broad daylight.

As a result of their disobedience, the pagan superpower Babylon—a sprawling empire which had grown mighty through God's sovereign permission—swooped down on his people and drove them like cattle into captivity.

What would the nations think about Israel's God now?

And what do they think about our God today—by watching us?

We've all made promises we haven't kept. That's why we can't look at Israel's captivity without seeing ourselves, without remembering the times when we too have been held hostage in our own forms of Babylon.

Yes, we are much alike. Just as God redeemed Israel from bondage in Egypt and established them as a "kingdom of priests," he has also redeemed us from slavery to sin and made us his kingdom people. Has this put a stop to our disobedience?

Just as the people responded to the conditions of God's covenant by saying, "We will do all that the LORD has spoken" (Exod. 19:8), we too have received God's Word and promised that we would faithfully obey it. Yet have we done so? Have we continued to follow him without question?

So we understand how it happens. We can relate to their short memory. We've all been there with them on the long march to Babylon, with God's blessings tossed unwanted at our backside and his corrective judgment staring us in the face. In revisiting, then, the events that led to Israel's captivity, we recall events that have cost us dearly in our own lives. And without making excuses or glossing over the details, we ask God to help us feel the gravity of this truth: *our disobedience profanes his holy name.*

THE COST OF DISOBEDIENCE

God had made a binding covenant with Israel and had fulfilled *his* part of the agreement in abundance. Yet Israel had failed to abide by theirs. And as a result, nearly the entire back half of the Old Testament is taken up with the fallout—God responding to a people he had blessed beyond measure yet who had failed him with repeated regularity. This is why he sent a long line of prophets to alert and alarm them, to help them see that the consequence of their failure was now being projected on an international scale.

Their disobedience was desecrating his name throughout the world.

Jeremiah was one of those prophets. He described the unfaithfulness of Israel as harlotry—spiritual adultery—and declared that God in his holiness and justice had given Israel a "certificate of divorce" (Jer. 3:8). They had rejected his law and failed to obey his voice, so God had scattered them among the nations, removing them for a time from the land of promise. What a contrast— a nation destined to be *sent* among the nations for God's "fame, praise, and glory" (Jer. 13:11), now *conquered* and *consumed* by the nations in defeat and disgrace.

You can hear the pain in Jeremiah's voice as he cries aloud to God: "You brought Your people Israel out of Egypt with signs and wonders, with a strong hand and an outstretched arm, and with great terror. You gave them this land You swore to give to their ancestors, a land flowing with milk and honey. They entered and possessed it, but"—*even after all of this*—"they did not obey Your voice or live according to Your law. They failed to perform all You commanded them to do, and so You have brought all this disaster on them" (Jer. 32:21–23).

God had been faithful to his promises all along. Yet Israel had ignored God's concern for the nations, had violated his covenant, and had profaned his name. So God also had to uphold the *hard* part of his covenant—punishing his own people for failing to do what he had commanded them, for failing to live out the responsibilities of his kingdom people.

Parents know this feeling. We've all experienced, to one extent or another, what it's like to give good gifts to our children only to receive in return their rebellion and disobedience. We could be tempted to let our kids slide by with their sins and slip-ups, to hope the problems go away and our family name doesn't risk being tarnished. But kingdom families—those who have been blessed by God to embody his name—must deal with the sin under their own rooftops, just as God in his holiness and justice had to punish his people for their disobedience.

This is not just the ancient past we're dealing with in this book, any more than God's kingdom is a tired theological concept that has no bearing on life outside the Bible. Do we not find ourselves at times, like disobedient children, presuming upon God's graciousness? Do we request and anticipate his blessing whether we're being obedient to his Word or not? What blessings are we sacrificing—and in turn withholding from others—by holding on to our own way so tightly?

Disobedience always comes with a multitude of bad consequences, one on top of the other. God loves us too much for our sin to do otherwise.

THE DOMINO EFFECT

Yes, disobedience has a domino effect. One domino topples into another, and before we know it, all the dominos are scattered about the table in complete disarray.

This is how it was in the life of Israel. As a result of their disobedience, the whole society had become sick unto death.

- While some people rolled in wealth and luxury, others in the covenant community lived in hopeless poverty.
- Though places of worship were busy and crowded with worshippers, the religion of the people had become mechanical and uninspired.
- Their inward lives—in spite of their overt religious activity—had become vilely corrupted by rampant greed and sexual impurity.[1]

Amos, another of God's brave, truth-telling prophets, stepped into the middle of this "what's wrong with this picture" environment, exposing a nation crushing the needy to pay for their own pleasures, selling "a righteous person for silver and a needy person for a pair of sandals" (Amos 2:6). He told of a man and his father having sex with the same woman, "profaning My holy name" and making a mockery of their outwardly religious show (Amos 2:7).

Isaiah, too, brought sins like these to light, pronouncing woe upon the people: "Woe to those enacting crooked statutes and writing oppressive laws to keep the poor from getting a fair trial and to deprive the afflicted among my people of justice, so that widows can be their spoil and they can plunder the fatherless" (Isa. 10:1–2).

From mild forms of disobedience had grown insane levels of hatred, distrust, and envy.

And worst of all, hypocrisy.

Long before Jesus would rail on the religious leaders of his day for their mistreatment of others in the name of religious purity, God the Father was condemning the hypocrisy of his people in the most swift and severe of terms. "I hate, I despise your feasts! I can't stand the stench of your solemn assemblies. Even if you offer Me your burnt offerings and grain offerings, I will not accept them; I will have no regard for your fellowship offerings of fattened cattle. Take away from Me the noise of your songs! I will not listen to the music of your harps. But let justice flow like water, and righteousness, like an unfailing stream" (Amos 5:21–24).

Words like these are painful to read, to hear, to imagine God saying. Yet these are merely a few of the indictments lifted by the lamenting voice of every Old Testament prophet—in order that God's name would no longer be profaned.

Sadly, however, their voice is still needed in our ears today. Much like ancient Israel, we can see the excessive material abundance in our society, even though vast pockets of the world—and even some within a few miles of our homes and churches—live in poverty and want. We are bombarded by sexual perversion on every hand, our television sets becoming a continuous flow of little else. Tales of injustice greet us each day in the newspaper, and yet such stories continue unabated, it seems, despite our awareness of the wrongs. Church attendance is growing, nearly exploding in many places, yet our culture remains just as sick as before—untouched, unfazed by the presence of kingdom people in its midst.

This should make us pause and ask ourselves about our own commitment to personal and corporate obedience. Are we and our churches actively hallowing the Lord's name by obeying his Word, or are we following in the steps of Israel—using religious activity to take the place of obedient holiness?

Truly, this domino effect of disobedience—so easy to see in others—is not always so easy to spot in ourselves.

GOD'S NAME AMONG THE NATIONS

The prophet Ezekiel was among those taken into Babylonian exile, and God used him to put this catastrophic event into historical perspective, helping his people see the astonishment their captivity had caused in the minds of the nations. As he wrote, "When [Israel] came to the nations where they went, they profaned My holy name, because it was said about them: 'These are the people of the LORD, yet they had to leave His land in exile'" (Ezek. 36:20).

The average citizen of Ezekiel's day often associated a deity with a specific land and people. So it's not hard to understand the conclusion drawn by the surrounding pagan nations: either Israel's God had abandoned his people, or he was incapable of defending them against Marduk, the god of Babylon. If God had indeed abandoned his people, then his credibility was seriously at stake. If not—and the god Marduk was simply more powerful than the God of Israel—then God was not as sovereign as he said he was.[2]

Either way God's name was being trampled underfoot.

Moses had seen this same thing coming in Israel's early days. He had understood from the beginning that the fate of God's people and the reputation of their God were inextricably linked together.

After the incident with the golden calf (Exod. 32), he begged God to relent from destroying his people, arguing that the Egyptians would conclude that God had led them out of bondage with an evil intent.

Later, when God's anger raged against Israel for believing the report of the lying spies and failing to enter the promised land, Moses again appealed to God on the basis of the impact the people's destruction would have on the Lord's name. "If You kill this people with a single blow, the nations that have heard of Your fame will declare, 'Since the LORD wasn't able to bring this people into the land He swore to give them, He has slaughtered them in the wilderness'" (Num. 14:15–16).

God's name is what matters. It stands for his own holy character. So those of us who embody his name do not merely represent ourselves and our families as we go about our daily lives. We kingdom people bear the name of our king.

And he takes his name very seriously.

But all is not lost if we've smeared God's name in the dust and dirt of our own disobedience. As we'll see in the next chapter, God has a way of restoring the glory and honor of his name, even after it's been soiled by our sin and insincerity.

Yes, because of the unfaithfulness of his people, we have allowed others—the ones God desires to worship him—to conclude falsely that he is no God at all.

Yet we can be sure that God will restore and renew us *for the sake of his name,* transforming us into people who wear his name well.

- Can nations change from evil to good as well as from good to evil?
- Can you think of a nation whose "name" has changed?
- When people hear your name, what image comes to their minds?
- Is this an image you want to maintain or one you'd like to change?

Chapter 10

GETTING HOLY THE HARD WAY

"I will honor the holiness of My great name, which has been profaned among the nations—the name you have profaned among them. The nations will know that I am Yahweh"— the declaration of the Lord GOD—"when I demonstrate My holiness through you in their sight."

EZEKIEL 36:23

HAVE YOU EVER HAD anyone question your integrity to such a degree that you really believed your reputation had been harmed?

Perhaps someone at work started a rumor or implied that you were less than honest. Perhaps someone at school suggested to a few other people that you weren't quite as pure and holy as you appear to be. Perhaps a friend at church misconstrued a comment you made in passing, and now you find yourself having to defend something you didn't even say.

When things like these happen to place our reputation in danger, we go straight to the ones who've heard the false accusations—the ones we want to respect us, the ones with whom that respect may be in jeopardy. These are the ones we want to assure of our innocence, those who live in the same arena where our good name was impugned.

God faced this same issue when Israel was taken into captivity in Babylon. Here they were, hauled away from their homeland because of their disobedience, his name profaned in a global arena. It would do little good to vindicate his reputation in some obscure corner of the world where few would see or notice the difference.

Yes, if God were going to establish his supremacy as the ruler of his people Israel and as the sovereign Lord over all, his deliverance was going to have to happen out in the open, where everyone who wondered at his power could witness it for themselves.

The nations needed to know. And God intended to show them. For his name's sake.

FOR US OR FOR HIM?

God had remained long-suffering with his people as they continued in rebellion. He warned them time and again that he would be forced to discipline them for their disobedience. And finally, after being repeatedly rebuffed and rejected, he allowed his people to be carried into captivity—to be punished, corrected, and restored. All of the things Israel could have enjoyed through simple obedience to God and his Word—freedom, wisdom, blessing, protection—they would now be forced to reclaim on the back end of his painful discipline.

So with his people scattered and displaced among a pagan nation—a nation he had chosen as his own instrument of divine judgment—God was preparing to come to their rescue and reestablish the awesome holiness of his name on the global stage . . . for their good and for his glory.

This is a key concept for kingdom people to remember. God acts in human history for our good and his glory. But lest we wonder which one of these is the more important of the two, let's settle this question in a hurry: God's glory always comes first.

For example, when God began to move on behalf of his people in Babylon, he made clear through the prophet Ezekiel that "it is not for your sake that I will act, house of Israel, but for My holy name, which you profaned among the nations where you went" (Ezek. 36:22).

Their deliverance was about God. *Everything* is about God. His desire—(I repeat this again, and kingdom people must embrace this mission as their own)—his desire is to see that the nations come to know him as the living God.

We, like Israel, are tempted to think that we are the center of the universe, that our desires determine God's agenda. Part of me wishes this were true. This kind of message has an immediate appeal and makes much more popular men out of us preachers. But when I consider the end result of this kind of theology—the self-centered emptiness of expecting God to bow to our personal wishes—I don't want any part of what it offers. It's like peeling away the layers of an onion, working our way further down into ourselves until there's nothing left to show for all of our struggle.

The sooner we understand that God is King—that he alone is the center of the universe—the sooner we'll come to experience the freedom of living in his kind of purpose and protection. It is indeed the only way to live.

God's character will always determine his activity. And because his desire is for the nations to know him as Lord, we will find our greatest good *only* in seeking his purposes.

Even if, like Israel, we have to learn them the hard way.

GOD'S OUTWARD CALL

This doesn't mean that we're each called by God to be missionaries to Africa (although some of us are)! Please don't be compulsive enough to feel like the weight of this task has fallen with full force on your shoulders. God himself is responsible for placing his people throughout the nations of the world, not us by ourselves.

But we should interpret this calling to the nations in terms of our love for other people—no matter where they are. Do we genuinely care about the people we meet each day—the way God cares about them? Are we concerned enough about their lostness to become involved in their lives? When missionaries come to our church to report on their ministry, do we consider it a good time to skip service? Does God's work in reaching the nations just not do it for us?

How do we really feel about the fate of the nations, about the *people* of the nations, about the people of *our* nation?

God is consumed with love for them. That's why he has called us into this royal priesthood—to perform the role of reaching the nations, of being his messengers in bringing redemption to others.

Since this is the last chapter in this section on "A King and His Purpose," I believe it is absolutely essential to cement this kingdom vision in our minds. It is the clear message of the Scripture, and I think it's important to let God's Word speak for itself. The cumulative effect of these verses is impressive indeed:

- "Sing a new song to the LORD; sing to the LORD, all the earth. Sing to the LORD, praise His name; proclaim His salvation from day to day. Declare His glory among the nations, His wonderful works among all peoples" (Ps. 96:1–3).

- "Ascribe to the LORD, families of the peoples, ascribe to the LORD glory and strength. Ascribe to the LORD the glory of His name; bring an offering and enter His courts. Worship the LORD in His holy majesty; tremble before Him, all the earth. Say among the nations: 'The LORD reigns'" (Ps. 96:7–10a).

- The writer of Psalm 102 composed his message as a prayer of hope to the Lord: "You will arise and have compassion on Zion, for it is time to show favor to her—the appointed time has come" (v. 13). Why should God extend such mercy and blessing to his people? Here's why: "Then the nations will fear the name of the LORD, and all the kings of the earth Your glory" (v. 15). The psalmist looked forward to a day "when peoples and kingdoms"—men and women of every tribe and tongue—"are assembled to serve the LORD" (v. 22).

- The prophet Isaiah, too, referred constantly to God's desire for the nations. When he spoke in advance of the liberation of Israel from captivity, he looked to a time when, not just Israel, but "everyone called by My name and created for My glory" would be gathered to the Lord (Isa. 43:7).

- In chapter 49 he compared Israel to a "sharpened arrow" God had hidden in his quiver (v. 2), created "from the womb to be His servant, to bring Jacob back to Him so that Israel might be gathered to Him" (v. 5). Yet in a surprising twist, Isaiah declared, "It is not enough for you to be My servant raising up the tribes of Jacob and restoring the protected ones of Israel. I will also make you a light for the nations, to be My salvation to the ends of the earth" (v. 6).

- Truly, "The LORD has displayed His holy arm in the sight of all the nations; all the ends of the earth will see the salvation of our God" (Isa. 52:10). God had one purpose in mind for vindicating his name: the redemption of the nations.

So we will either embrace this mission along with him, through the preferred path of our willful trust and obedience, or God will take whatever means necessary to ensure that our lives are purified to perform his kingdom purpose.

Neither path is simple, but it's one or the other for kingdom people. And no path is so treacherously difficult as the one that always ends in the Lord's punishment and correction.

THE PURPOSE OF REPENTANCE

When God restores us to right relationship with him, when he draws us away from our disobedience and toward himself, when he lets us taste the sourness our sin has brought upon us and makes us want to serve him again, he does this not merely to help us sleep better at night and go to church in a holier mood. When in our weakness he makes us strong, he does so to give us firsthand experiences we can share with others. When he reminds us through times of punishment and judgment that he truly is the only way to peace and contentment, he intends for us to communicate this message to the people he places in our path. Like them, we've tried going around God's Word and seeing if we can't live without him for a while. But just like every time before, we've discovered anew that he's all we really have. He's all we really need.

It's not as though we're being saved all over again, and yet it brings the reality of our salvation totally up-to-date and fresh in our minds—God's coming to our rescue when we were unable to help ourselves. It jars us back into the stark reality that everyone we meet is in need of this transforming truth.

It gives us back our kingdom focus.

The redemption of Israel was designed to vindicate God's name among the nations—just as his ongoing acts of mercy in our own lives are designed to honor his name among the people in our midst.

When the nations saw his might and knew that he had not failed his people Israel, the whole world was reminded again that this God truly was sovereign and all-powerful. When Israel broke down in repentance and experienced sorrow for their sins, his holiness shone through their lives and caught the attention of all who knew them.

He does the same with us.

Perhaps you have gone through a season of serious rebellion at some point in your life. For a long stretch of time, you ran from God and discounted the Christian life as something that didn't seem worth the trouble. You knew in your heart that his Word was probably right, but you wanted to try things your own way for a while. Somewhere along the way, however, life came down hard on your self-made plans, and whatever freedom you thought you were chasing turned its teeth on you and shocked you into repentance.

We've all experienced some version of this story. The details are different, but the result is the same. God has delivered us so that we could tell this story, so that we could go to those who have seen his name profaned in our lives, so that we could show them what happens when this loving God reaches out to rescue his children and vindicate his holy name.

"I will not keep silent because of Zion," the prophet Isaiah said, "and I will not keep still because of Jerusalem until her righteousness shines like a bright light, and her salvation like a flaming torch" (Isa. 62:1). It's like Paul's admonition to the Ephesian believers that they "walk as children of light" (Eph. 5:8), or his challenge to the Philippians that they be "blameless and pure, children of God who are faultless in a crooked and perverted generation, among whom you shine like stars in the world" (Phil. 2:15).

Our holiness will always mark us as someone who has been with God, and it will enable us to have an effective witness for him in our world—even when God has had to win our obedience the hard way.

This is the purpose of the King.

• What evidence do you see that people in your city or community care/don't care about other people?

- Do you think your community or city is the same or different from other parts of this country?
- What evidence can you find in your own life that you care about people?

SECTION 3

His Kingdom Comes

Chapter 11

GETTING YOUR STRENGTH BACK

"I will give you a new heart and put a new spirit within you; I will remove your heart of stone and give you a heart of flesh."

EZEKIEL 36:26

THE LAST TWO CHAPTERS have dealt with some hard realities of kingdom living—the cost of disobedience and the reach of God's judgment. Yet even in the face of punishment and regret, we have seen signs of life, signs of hope, signs of purpose in the midst of pain.

This, too, is God's heart.

Yes, Israel's vital signs during the long, lonely years of exile had become weak and unstable. They realized they had ignored the warnings of the prophets who had diagnosed the dangerous extent of Israel's heart condition. They knew they had disobeyed God and had stubbornly sat by while their hearts were turning to stone. They were aware that their national upheaval, their loss of freedom—their spiritual heart attack—had been the result of many years of rebellion. Babylonian captivity had indeed been a humbling blow, and Israel was now struggling for its survival.

But God's kingdom shines in moments like these—just when its enemies think they've slammed its doors shut for good.

So in the midst of this crisis context, with Israel at its lowest ebb, the prophet Ezekiel stepped forward and declared God's intention to revive his people, to rally his kingdom. Many years before, of course, God had redeemed Israel from Egypt. And by his transforming power they had emerged not as a loose collection of families but as a nation, a kingdom of priests.

And he was about to do it again.

The long night in Babylon would mark another turning point in the life of Israel. They had been taken into captivity a proud nation, but they would emerge as a new spiritual entity, a revitalized remnant that would return home with a new and responsive heart, a transformed people who would possess God's Spirit within them.

It's not exaggerating the point to suggest that what we are witnessing here is the beginning of the New Testament church, God's messianic community. We are witnessing God's kingdom rousing from the appearance of sleep, yet marching (as always) to the beat of God's sovereign purpose and perfect timing.

We are witnessing what happens when God revives us from our rebellion.

THE PROMISE OF RESTORATION

God's plan to vindicate his name among the nations began with the physical act of restoring the exiles to the promised land, a place that was hardly a mere geographic destination for the Jewish people. This homeland was at the heart of their life and worship. That's why their return had been a constant theme of the Old Testament.

Moses had even spoken of this homecoming as far back as the book of Deuteronomy. Though his original hearers couldn't possibly have grasped the larger, historical significance of what he was saying, Moses told them that God would "restore your fortunes, have compassion on you, and gather you again from all the peoples where the LORD your God has scattered you. Even if your exiles are at the ends of the earth, He will gather you and bring you back from there" (Deut. 30:3–4).

None of this had caught God by surprise.

Nehemiah himself quoted from this same prophetic text after receiving news of his people's suffering in Jerusalem. The exiles who had returned home were finding the going rough. Their city lay in ruins. And though he lived far away at the time from the land of his fathers, Nehemiah prayed in anguish to the Lord before returning to rebuild the walls. "Please remember what You commanded Your servant Moses: 'If you are unfaithful, I will scatter you among the peoples. But if you return to Me and carefully observe My commands, even though your exiles were banished to the ends of the earth, I will gather them from there and bring them to the place where I chose to have My name dwell'" (Neh. 1:8–9).

The day of restoration had come. God's redemptive plan for the nations would not fail, even though the nation of Israel had failed to be faithful to the covenant.

He would raise up for himself a people who would possess his word in their hearts, not just on their lips—a people who would house God's Spirit inside them, not just down the road at God's house.

Yes, revival always begins with a righteous remnant.

We see this truth coming to vivid life in the prophecy of Ezekiel, through words and phrases that still have the power to reach into our living rooms and renew our troubled souls. When we hear him speaking to the people of Israel, promising them God's cleansing, his renewal, his empowerment, and his restoration to fruitful ministry, we can feel our own sins falling away, the tug of temptation loosening its grip, and our spirits taking deep breaths of hope, vision, and freshness.

This is the kingdom talking. This is the power of God rushing through our veins, restoring the blood flow to our weak and damaged arteries, performing his sovereign act of revival so that his kingdom work can pour forth from us in power.

Tell us, Ezekiel, what our tired souls need to hear.

I WILL CLEANSE YOU

It's not enough for us to be rescued from our sins, to be pulled from harm's way and returned to safety. We must also be renewed. The promise of restoration comes hand in hand with a moral and spiritual change of heart.

So God told his people Israel that they must be purified from the filthy buildup caused by their rebellion and idolatry. Ezekiel used the terminology of sprinkling with clean water (Ezek. 36:25), a reference to the ritual washings intended to remove ceremonial uncleanness from the people. But this sprinkling is much more than a lick and a promise we slap on ourselves. This is something only God can do, a deep cleansing action that sets us free from the guilt our disobedience has caused.

God's demands for holiness and purity have not changed in the time since Ezekiel spoke these words. And if we desire restoration today in our own lives and churches, we too must allow the Father to cleanse us from our filthiness.

Study after study has indicated that the lifestyles of many who claim to be Christians are so similar to that of the world, our witness is being dulled by the compromise. We are desperately in need of this cleansing of our hearts and minds. The formula for it has never changed: we must turn from our wickedness in true humility and allow God's Word to purify us. Just as Jesus asked the Father to sanctify the disciples with the truth of his Word (John 17:17), we too must seek the deep cleansing of God—if we are serious about being kingdom people.

I WILL GIVE YOU A NEW HEART

When God brings restoration to his people, he doesn't stop with the cleansing part. He doesn't just remove our sin. He also heals and revives. He performs radical surgery on us, enabling his people to live in obedience to his Word. He gives us a "new heart" and a "new spirit," removing our "heart of stone" and giving us a "heart of flesh" (Ezek. 36:26)—a heart that's alive and healthy and thriving.

The heart is not just one individual part of a person's makeup. It comprises our total personality. We use the term *heart* to refer to our mind, will, and emotions. It stands for the seat of our personality.

Jesus, you remember, called the scribes and Pharisees "hypocrites" because they honored him with their lips "but their heart is far from Me" (Matt. 15:7–8, quoting from Isa. 29:13). These men, unrivaled in their obsession with ceremonial purity, were greatly offended by this statement. Christ's disciples, too, appeared somewhat shocked by his implication. Didn't Jesus know that these men to whom he was speaking so harshly had every appearance of holiness and uprightness? Yes, but Jesus knew more. He knew their "evil thoughts, murders, adulteries, sexual immoralities, thefts, false testimonies, blasphemies," and all the rest, and he knew where these secret sins came from. "From the heart" come the things that truly define a person. Our hearts tell us who we really are.

Israel's heart had become like fossilized stone, unfeeling and unresponsive. But God promised to do for them what they could not do for themselves. He said he would give them a heart of flesh, a heart he could mold and move and fashion, a heart that could hear his Word and react in obedience.

Do you sometimes feel like you have a heart of stone? When you read the Scripture, does it almost always seem dull and irrelevant? Do you find yourself fidgeting most Sundays during worship while those around you are enjoying the presence of God?

Then you, like all us at one time or another, are in desperate need of a heart transplant. But you've come to the right place because the only one able to perform this delicate operation is already here in the room, eager to hear your cry for help, ready to make you new and alive inside . . . again.

I WILL PUT MY SPIRIT WITHIN YOU

God's promises just seem to get better and better. Not only was Israel set to receive a new heart and a new spirit, but God also promised, "I will place My Spirit within you." This implanting of God's uncreated Spirit inside of them would transform their motives, enabling them "to follow My statutes and carefully observe My ordinances" (Ezek. 36:27).

The promises of God's covenant had been based on Israel's obedience to his Word. But their struggle to obey the law demonstrated that the human heart is wicked, that we in our own strength cannot keep the law of God. We need cleansing. We need our hearts reset, restored, and revived. But we need more than that.

We need God's Spirit. We not only need our *own* lives recharged and recalibrated. *We also need God's life inside of us,* his eternal Holy Spirit.

There's no other way to live the kingdom life.

Kingdom people don't pull themselves up by their own bootstraps. They submit themselves to God and give his power a clear, obedient path to surge through.

Ezekiel wasn't the only prophet who spoke of a day when obedience would flow from God through willing hearts. Jeremiah also described this new covenant reality: "This is the covenant I will make with the house of Israel after those days"—the LORD's declaration. "I will place My law within them and write it on their hearts. I will be their God, and they will be My people. No longer will one teach his neighbor or his brother, saying: Know the LORD, for they will all know Me, from the least to the greatest of them"—the LORD's declaration. "For I will forgive their wrongdoing and never again remember their sin" (Jer. 31:33–34).

We are the recipients of this new covenant. God has written his law on our hearts, and he has endowed our lives with his Spirit. These prophetic Scriptures were a sign that the messianic age was dawning, a time when God would "pour water on the thirsty land, and streams on the dry ground," when he would "pour out My Spirit on your descendants and My blessing on your offspring" (Isa. 44:3). It foretold of a coming One who would have "My Spirit on Him" (Isa. 42:1) and would empower the people of his kingdom to obey his word and experience his full blessing.

Though already present in reality, the kingdom was coming in force.

And God's Spirit would drive it right into our lives.

I WILL DO IT ALL

God went on to promise even more in this passage from Ezekiel 36:

1. *He promised permanence.* God said that his people would "live in the land" (v. 28). They would not just return and stay for a few years. They would dwell there, abide there. By cleansing Israel from impurity and giving them his Spirit, he would empower them to remain lastingly pure—to establish a habitual pattern of obedience.

2. *He promised growth and supply.* God said he would "summon the grain and make it plentiful," to make "the fruit of the trees and the produce of the field plentiful, so that you will no longer experience reproach among the nations on account of

famine" (vv. 29–30). Land that was once desolate would "become like the garden of Eden" (v. 35). This remains his promise to us. Though our lives and our churches can languish for years in disuse and decay, God's Spirit can breathe new life into the dusty corridors of our hearts. He can refresh and replenish. He can make us useful, thriving people in his kingdom. This, I promise you, is your Father's desire for you.

3. *He promised the spread of his kingdom.* His desire in redeeming us, as always, is to extend his kingdom's reach to others. Beginning in Ezekiel 36:30 and stretching to the end of the chapter, you'll discover four specific references to *the nations,* the sum being that "the nations that remain around you will know that I, the LORD, have rebuilt what was destroyed and have replanted what was desolate. I, the LORD, have spoken and I will do it" (v. 36). God wants to bring revival and fruitfulness to you and your church for a singular purpose—that the nations "will know that I am the LORD" (v. 38).

We ask him to start with us—to do in our lives what he did in the valley of dry bones, the vision which immediately follows in Ezekiel 37. "Can these bones live?" the Lord asked the prophet. "Lord GOD, only You know" was Ezekiel's wise reply (v. 3). And by the breath of God—the Spirit of God—these chalky, discarded remains of past defeats and ruined potential began retaking form and shape and sinew. "They came to life and stood on their feet, a vast army" (v. 10)—renewed to march again at the orders of their King.

Do you see yourself in this army? Can you feel yourself being shaken from the sleep of sin and death and reestablished as an able foot soldier in God's calling to the nations? Will you let his

Spirit, not your own guts and willpower, animate your actions as you head into today and tomorrow?

This is the way—the only way—kingdom people get their strength back.

- Do you need a new heart? Do you want to restore your relationship with God? What will you do to get a new heart?
- Is your life desolate or fruitful? If fruitful, what fruit is evident as a result of your relationship with God?

Chapter 12

STARTING FRESH

"In those days Judah will be saved, and Jerusalem will dwell securely, and this is what she will be named: The LORD Is Our Righteousness. For this is what the LORD says: David will never fail to have a man sitting on the throne of the house of Israel."

JEREMIAH 33:16–17

IF YOU'RE A FOOTBALL FAN, you've undoubtedly seen a play develop that was an absolute disconnect. The quarterback expected his receiver to break for the end zone, but instead he pulled up short. The pass, timed to hit the receiver in stride, sailed far over his head, incomplete—or worse, intercepted. Because of the receiver's lack of understanding or poor execution, the result was a busted play.

The nation of Israel had experienced a disconnect like this in their covenant relationship with God. He had redeemed them and chosen them for himself. He had set them among the nations for his glory and praise, so that people of all races and backgrounds might share in his kingdom. He had given Israel his Word to help them live in a manner that would display his character, allowing the nations to see his righteousness.

But they had turned the opposite way. Their behavior, rather than honoring his name, had profaned his name. They had felt entitled to God's blessings and, instead of sharing them with the nations, had hoarded for themselves the privilege of relationship with him. Though God had intended that his people *convey* these blessings to others, they had *consumed* them as a birthright. We've seen this lived out over and over again as we've tracked Israel's walk through the Old Testament.

"I spoke to you when you were secure," the Lord said through the prophet Jeremiah. But "you said: I will not listen. This has been your way since youth; indeed, you have never listened to Me" (Jer. 22:21).

He goes on.

"Time and time again I have sent you all My servants the prophets, proclaiming: Turn, each one from his evil way of life, and correct your actions. Stop following other gods to serve them. Live in the land that I gave you and your ancestors. But you would not pay attention or obey Me" (Jer. 35:15).

In the end—as we have seen in the last few chapters—God chose the long way around to restore his people: captivity in Babylon. But their exile—far from being the dying breath of God's kingdom activity—became by his grace a time of spiritual renewal and hope.

Although it's true that the prophets nearly set the people's ears afire with their blunt indictments of Israel's disobedience, they also looked to the future, painting a picture whose glory seemed impossible to imagine in the face of such circumstances. They saw the restoration of a righteous remnant. They saw a new covenant, even stronger than before, being forged in the fire of judgment. They saw all of history moving relentlessly in the direction of God's kingdom.

They saw a promise of hope.

They saw a fresh start for his people.

They saw . . . a Messiah.

ISRAEL'S FAILURE

It has often been said that when we ignore the lessons of history, we are doomed to repeat the failures of the past. So it's important—before looking too far ahead—that we summarize why Israel failed in their calling to be a kingdom people.

1. *They failed to embrace his mission.* God's desire had always been to use his people as a platform to win worshippers from other nations. Israel disregarded this clear commission—much as we do by soaking up God's blessings, by keeping his Word to ourselves, by evaluating our church services by how well they feed us.

2. *They failed to embody his name.* They had turned the concept of the kingdom of *God* into the kingdom of *Israel*. They lived for their own glory rather than the glory of the Father. They were more enamored of their own *place* in history than they were of God's *purpose* for them in history. We as God's people of today cannot afford to repeat this fatal error. John Bright asks, "Will we, like Israel, imagine that our destiny under God and God's purposes in history are to be realized in terms of the society we have built? The temptation to do so is subtle. After all, we may claim a Christian heritage from which human liberties have flowed."[1]

3. *They failed to be obedient to God's Word.* This was at the heart of their demise. It led to behavioral issues that impacted their holiness, which in turn negated any witness they might have had to the nations. We must learn from this. The Bible still remains an unopened mystery to too many believers. And even

those of us who know it well are often guilty of compromising its teachings and twisting it in the direction of ourselves and our interests. Our lives must be *in* and *about* the Word of God.

To *embrace* his mission, *embody* his name, and *obey* his Word is the calling of every kingdom person. To fail in these areas is to risk the ineffective fate of ancient Israel.

THE RETURN OF THE REMNANT

To realize in honesty and humility that we haven't always been faithful to these callings—and to want them restored to us with all our heart and soul—is to feel the fresh start of the righteous remnant.

When the prophets spoke of the remnant's return, they not only injected hope into the midst of deep darkness but also projected kingdom thinking into the future. Instead of the nation of Israel remaining the sole recipients of the covenant, the kingdom activity of God shifted to a new ground of operations—a righteous remnant chosen by God to reflect his name and purpose.

The kingdom shifted to us.

John Bright boldly and correctly sees in the promise of this remnant the seeds of the New Testament church. Speaking of the prophets who came after Isaiah, he writes: "They all understood that a new Israel 'according to the spirit,' not the nation Israel, would be heir of the promise of the Kingdom. In all of them the notion of the Remnant appears, even where the term is not used. It is precisely as this new Israel . . . that the New Testament church understood itself."[2]

Watch as this distinction begins to build. In Jeremiah 24, the prophet pictured the exiles as being like two baskets of figs—both good and bad. The bad figs—"so bad they are inedible"—were to be made "an object of horror and disaster to all the kingdoms of the earth" (vv. 8–9). The good figs, however, were to be returned to the land—to be built up and not demolished, to be planted and never again uprooted. Even more importantly, God said, "I will give them a heart to know Me, that I am the LORD. They will be My people, and I will be their God because they will return to Me with all their heart" (v. 7).

Jeremiah, able to see all of this with kingdom vision, rejoiced in God's goodness, in his merciful, miraculous plan to extend his covenant blessings into eternity—even though Jeremiah knew it would anger and aggravate many who failed to grasp what God was doing. "'For I know the plans I have for you'—this is the LORD's declaration—'plans for your welfare, not for disaster, to give you a future and a hope'" (Jer. 29:11).

He properly understood the impact this restoration would have on the surrounding nations and on God's kingdom purposes for his people. "Nations, hear the word of the LORD, and tell it among the far off coastlands! Say: The One who scattered Israel will gather him. He will watch over him as a shepherd guards his flock, for the LORD has ransomed Jacob and redeemed him from the power of one stronger than he" (Jer. 31:10–11). God's gathering of his righteous remnant would demonstrate to the world both his faithfulness and his authority, matters brought into question by the lifestyle of his people and their accompanying captivity.

The prophecy of Ezekiel is also taken up with this image of God as a shepherd gathering his scattered flock, his chosen remnant. "For this is what the Lord GOD says: See, I Myself will search for My flock and look for them. As a shepherd looks for his sheep on the day he is among his scattered flock, so I will look for My flock. I will rescue them from all the places where they have been scattered on a cloudy and dark day. I will bring them out from the peoples, gather them from the countries, and bring them into their own land. I will shepherd them on the mountains of Israel, in the ravines, and in all the inhabited places of the land" (Ezek. 34:11–13).

Ah, the personal care of the Lord. It should wrap us in gratitude and the full assurance of our protection in his arms. He walks among his sheep, caring for us, feeding us, and shielding us from danger. To those of us who are broken, he promises to bind up our wounds. To those of us who are sick, he promises to nourish and strengthen (v. 16).

Yet judgment awaits the fat sheep who once fed in good pasture, who have trampled its green freshness underfoot and muddied the clear water with their feet (vv. 17–19). Could this be a reference to those in Israel who had consumed God's blessing with no regard for the nations? These ungrateful, unresponsive breakers of God's covenant would be judged, the Lord said, and not restored.

But we cannot claim, as Israel did, God's blessings as our entitlements. Every time I read this passage from Ezekiel 34, I am convicted by what little we have done with the abundance God has given to the church in North America, what small amounts of our God-given wealth we have expended on reaching the nations. Are we at risk of becoming the "fat" sheep who trample his green pastureland and foul the water for others? How much of our church's time and energy are directed toward seeking the lost? What percentage of our church's budget is allocated not inward toward ourselves but outward to reach the nations?

The remnant's return from captivity was indeed a reason for true rejoicing. But the remnant's role in history—yes, the church's role in God's plan for the ages—is a reason for kingdom responsibility.

THE PROMISE OF THE MESSIAH

But we do not go alone into this kingdom mission because we have . . . him.

We have Jesus.

He is our fresh start for every day.

The remnant returning from exile certainly needed a fresh start. Their king, the one who carried David's royal blood in his veins, had been led away in disgrace into Babylon. To the people living in this historical context, the ancient prophecies that said David's "house and kingdom will endure before Me forever" and his "throne will be established forever" seemed a cruel lie, straight out of the mouth of God (2 Sam. 7:16).

Unless . . .

And it was this "unless"—this new revelation of God, this new way of interpreting the prophecies—that brought the expectation of a coming Messiah into sharper and sharper focus in the years following the exile.

"'The days are coming'—this is the LORD's declaration— 'when I will raise up a righteous Branch of David. He will reign wisely as king and administer justice and righteousness in the land. In His days Judah will be saved, and Israel will dwell securely.

This is what He will be named: The Lord Is Our Righteousness'" (Jer. 23:5–6).

"The Lord is Our Righteousness" translates as Jehovah Tsidkenu. There is a striking similarity between the name Tsidkenu and Zedekiah, the Israelite king who had brazenly ignored Jeremiah's warning about the nation's disobedience and the coming captivity. Actually, it was King Nebuchadnezzar of Babylon who had changed this king of Israel's name from Matthaniah to Zedekiah, a name meaning "the righteousness of Yahweh." More than likely he had done this as a way of scoffing at Israel's God and humiliating Israel's people. Yet little did Babylon's ruler know that a King *was* coming—infinitely mightier than the great Nebuchadnezzar—who truly *would be* the righteousness of God.[3]

The Messiah.

Jeremiah shouted this welcome news to the weary-eyed inhabitants of burned-out Jerusalem. Though the task of rebuilding on old promises seemed daunting indeed, the Lord guaranteed "this city will bear on My behalf a name of joy, praise, and glory before all the nations of the earth, who will hear of all the good I will do for them" (Jer. 33:9a). "In this place which you say is a ruin, without man or beast—that is, in Judah's cities and Jerusalem's streets that are a desolation without man, without inhabitant, and without beast—there will be heard again a sound of joy and gladness, the voice of the bridegroom and the bride, and the voice of those saying, 'Praise the LORD of Hosts, for the LORD is good; His faithful love endures forever'" (Jer. 33:10–11a).

The King was coming to fulfill all righteousness, to reestablish covenant continuity out of seeming chaos, to give God's people—

his righteous remnant—a fresh and glorious start. Yes, David's royal line may have had all the appearances of being chopped off at the stump, but look—there was Holy Spirit life in this family tree yet. Out of nowhere, a shoot was starting to grow (Isa. 11:1), planted by the One who had put these roots in the ground to begin with.

This kingdom doesn't die, because its King lives forever.

A fresh start is just around every kingdom corner.

A collapse in morals also creates a financial collapse. A generation ago marriage was the bedrock of family security. Today 50-plus percent of all marriages end in divorce, and most failed marriages are the result of financial problems or unfaithfulness. (Source: Baptist Press)

- In people you know, is their a link between moral failure and financial collapse?
- If life offered "do overs," what in your life would you change?
- Do you know anyone who seems to be "hopeful"? Do you know why?

Chapter 13

THE KING IS COMING

In those days John the Baptist came,
preaching in the wilderness of Judea and saying,
"Repent, because the kingdom of heaven has come near!"

MATTHEW 3:1–2

SOMETIMES AN ENTIRE COURT CASE is built around one person's testimony. The opposing attorneys badger the one witness from all sides, trying to raise doubts in the jury's minds about his authenticity, forcing them to question—in the absence of supporting testimony—whether one person's word is really enough to go on.

But when *several* witnesses exist to bear record to a certain event, the dynamics are a bit different. With various versions of testimony to hear and consider, the attorneys who are trying to prove the case must work hard to establish the credibility of the witnesses' stories. They must demonstrate a pattern of consistency to their testimonies, a common thread that runs throughout each one of them, even when told from a different perspective or viewpoint. When all of the witnesses give their accounts, and all of their testimonies point to the same conclusion, the lawyers feel pretty sure they have a winning case.

This is exactly what we see happening at the beginning of the New Testament—a wide range of witnesses from various places and backgrounds, some of them about as different from one another as they could possibly be, yet declaring messages so similar in substance and content, the truth of their claims seemed hard to disprove.

God was once again declaring the coming of his kingdom—here, there, and everywhere.

It had been more than four hundred years since people had been talking like this. In the time since the last prophetic voice of the Old Testament had laid down his fiery pen, Persia's King Cyrus had overthrown the Babylonian Empire. And under his rule those Jews who desired to do so had been allowed to return to Jerusalem where they rebuilt the walls and—eventually—the temple. Jewish religion and life had been reestablished.

Along the way the Greeks had enjoyed their season of world domination—including control of the land of Israel. This new oppression had taken some of the messianic wind out of the sails, which had been raised and stretched taut by the later prophets. But when the Maccabean revolt wrestled Israel free from the Greeks and their pagan deities in the mid-160s B.C., messianic excitement reached a new fever pitch.

Not for long, however.

Just as rapidly as their hopes had risen, internal conflicts and confusion brought this brief window of optimism to a close. The Romans stepped into the leadership vacuum, occupying the land of Israel (Palestine, by this time), riddling them with high taxes, and placing unstable, immoral rulers in authority.[1]

During the dead weight of these tumultuous years, God began sending his witnesses into the courtroom of common culture and giving his kingdom a name and face.

MATTHEW'S TESTIMONY

Matthew's Gospel begins with these words: "The historical record of Jesus Christ, the Son of David, the Son of Abraham" (Matt. 1:1), followed by a long list of name-begat-names. This may seem like a big waste of ink and effort to us. But to the Jews lineage was a matter of crucial importance. Matthew knew this, and he used his genealogy to establish several key issues:

1. *Kingdom continuity.* By placing the arrival of Jesus squarely into the stream of Old Testament history, he demonstrated the consistency in God's redemptive, kingdom design.

2. *Covenant promise.* His reference to Jesus as the "Son of David" and the "Son of Abraham" helped his readers see Christ as the fulfillment of the covenant. God was keeping his word. David's kingdom was indeed being established forever.

3. *Divine purpose.* By dividing the genealogy into three sections of fourteen, he revealed the deliberate order of God's plan and design, giving evidence that this precise moment was Christ's appointed time in history.

4. *Jewish heritage.* This family record revealed that Jesus' lineage tracked through the royal line of Judah. Matthew was establishing Jesus' status as king of the Jews.[2]

But it wasn't merely select Jews like Matthew who were noticing Jesus' importance and the coming of his kingdom. How about the wise men—pagan astrologers drawn to his birthplace by a star in the East? How about Herod, the Roman ruler in charge of the region of Jesus' birth, who was troubled enough by the rumors of this so-called "King of the Jews" that he did his best to put a stop to him? (Matt. 2:1–18).

The word was getting out. And the Word was making waves.

Yes, God had revealed to Matthew that Jesus truly was the Messiah, the delegated King of God's eternal kingdom. That's why this "kingdom of heaven" theme runs the length and breadth of Matthew's Gospel, pointing repeatedly to Jesus as the One sent by God himself to establish his kingdom on the earth. "The phrase 'the kingdom of God' therefore, points not to a specific situation or event but to 'God in control,' with all the breadth of meaning that phrase could cover."[3]

The King was coming.

MARY'S TESTIMONY

God revealed this news most incredibly, of course, to Mary— this fact that the child he had placed in her "will be great and will be called the Son of the Most High, and the Lord God will give Him the throne of His father David. He will reign over the house of Jacob forever, and His kingdom will have no end" (Luke 1:32–33).

Mary's response to her unusual, unexpected role in this kingdom event was one of questions, yes; dizzy bewilderment, surely—yet complete obedience and worship. When she shared this astounding news with her friend Elizabeth, Mary broke forth into prophetic praise (Luke 1:46–55).

The King was coming.

It must have seemed strange that after such a long period of prophetic drought, God would choose to speak some of his first words of new covenant promise through a poor peasant maid. Yet even the most humble and lowly among us can be full participants in the kingdom of God, turning our focus—like Mary—not on our own state or condition, but on the power of his messianic deliverance and on the power of his all-sufficient grace and mercy in the lives of everyone we meet.

ZACHARIAH'S TESTIMONY

Zachariah, you remember, was just minding his own business in the sanctuary of the Lord, burning an incense offering for the people and praying for the messianic redemption of Israel—just as he was supposed to do. But the ordinary and routine suddenly became rare and angelic, as Gabriel announced to him the coming of a son who would have a very special job to do.

This boy of his would be "filled with the Holy Spirit while still in his mother's womb"—old and barren though she was (or at least had always been up till now). He would "turn many of the sons of Israel to the Lord their God . . . the hearts of fathers to their children, and the disobedient to the understanding of the righteous, to make ready for the Lord a prepared people" (Luke 1:15–17).

Zachariah, himself filled with the Holy Spirit, began to prophesy. He praised God for this miraculous visitation, for answering their prayer for redemption by raising up a King from the house of David, for remembering the covenant he swore to Abraham, and for promising deliverance—not just political freedom but eternal salvation—to all those who would serve him "in holiness and righteousness" (Luke 1:75).

The King was coming.

And Zachariah's miracle baby would be in charge of telling the world.

JOHN THE BAPTIST'S TESTIMONY

We dealt with John the Baptist's kingdom message in the first chapter, but it's important to see it again here in context. His prophetic passion still screams for attention across the years: "Repent, because the kingdom of heaven has come near!" (Matt. 3:2)—the same words Jesus would use in defining his own purpose and call to action.

This connecting of *repentance* and the *kingdom* in the same sentence made clear that this kingdom was a spiritual one, not a shortcut to political self-rule and supremacy. The radical response of repentance—of turning away from sin and turning full tilt toward God—was absolutely necessary in order for us to participate in this coming kingdom, this kingdom "at hand." The perfect tense nature of this phrase—"at hand"—suggested that this was a state of affairs which had already begun and therefore demanded radical and immediate action.

The King was coming.

His people had to get ready.

SIMEON'S TESTIMONY

The next witness who stepped onto the stage of redemptive history is largely unknown to us. We are told only three things about him. He was "righteous and devout, looking forward to Israel's consolation, and the Holy Spirit was upon him" (Luke 2:25). "The consolation of Israel" is another way to refer to the coming of the Messiah.

He wasn't just casually letting the promises of God pick him up on days of worship, like people who hardly give a thought to God except on Sunday mornings. No, he could sense that the Messiah was near, close at hand. He knew the kingdom was somewhere in sight and that he would get a good look at it before he died. The Holy Spirit had promised him as much.

Simeon was one of those "movable possessions" we talked about in chapter 4, a person who was always in God's place at God's time. He came into the temple at the very moment that Mary and Joseph arrived to circumcise their son. Recognizing the child as his Savior, he took Jesus up in his arms and began to bless God.

Simeon's words, too, came out in prophetic song, celebrating his joy at witnessing the Lord's salvation. Yet his song also carried a striking note of universal rule—the fact that this chosen One would be "a light for revelation to the Gentiles and glory to Your people Israel" (Luke 2:32).

God's *glory* stands for the manifestation of himself—the revelation of his nature and character. This, you'll recall, was the reason God had chosen Israel as his covenant nation in the first place—to express his glory to the nations. This would never have diminished Israel's glory but would rather have brought it to full realization. They would have discovered their full worth by living out God's kingdom purpose.

But now God had chosen *his Son* to express his glory—both to those in Israel who would receive him by faith and to those out-side of Israel who would be part of God's righteous remnant.

The King was coming . . . to bring salvation to all men.

ANNA'S TESTIMONY

Anna, the prophetess, was eighty-four years old when we meet her in Luke 2:36–38. After her husband's death many years earlier, she had dedicated herself to worship with "fastings and prayers" (Luke 2:37). This was a disciplined, highly spiritual woman.

At the crucial moment after Simeon's testimony, Anna moved to center stage. She too was one of God's servants "looking for-ward to the redemption of Jerusalem" (Luke 2:38), aware of the presence of God's kingdom activity, aware of this truth that escaped many others grown old and tired of waiting: the King was coming.

A CONTINUAL TESTIMONY PHASE

And the list of witnesses just continued to increase and branch out, covering all ages and nations and socioeconomic situations. Widows and orphans. High stations and hard laborers. Jews and Gentiles.

At the foot of the cross, for example, a Roman military officer voiced his unavoidable conclusion after watching Jesus die in humble obedience to the Father. "This man really was God's Son!" (Mark 15:39).

Later that evening, Joseph of Arimathea—one of the select seventy-one members of the Sanhedrin, the highest Jewish coun-cil of the first century—gathered up his courage and requested the body of Jesus from Pilate. Why would this wealthy Jew risk the scorn of his colleagues? The text tells it all: "[He] was himself looking forward to the kingdom of God" (Mark 15:43)—like Simeon, like Anna, like all the others.

You couldn't assemble a more diverse group of witnesses. Yet their stories and testimonies held true across the board. They all had one central thing in common.

They were looking for the kingdom of God!

And today God is looking for even more men and women, young and old, who will be like these faithful agents in his kingdom activity.

Will you be the next one to step onto the stage?

Will you be the one who's always watching for the situations where God's kingdom activity is taking place?

Will you do your part in advancing his kingdom?

Your King has come!

- What have you seen change in the world that you never expected to see? What nations or businesses or institutions have collapsed? Have any of these affected you personally? How did the collapse make you feel?
- In the midst of constant change, where do you find security?
- Does the continuity of God's kingdom offer security for you?

Chapter 14

MAN'S GLORY
OR GOD'S KINGDOM?

*Again, the Devil took Him to a very high mountain and showed Him
all the kingdoms of the world and their splendor.*

MATTHEW 4:8

I'D GUESS IN YOUR LIFETIME you've probably heard two
dozen sermons or more on the temptation or testing of Jesus. It's
a natural text for preachers. It comes complete with a three-point
outline. It prints out the Old Testament cross-references right
there in the Gospels so you don't even have to ask people to look
them up. It has imagery, it has action, it even has a happy ending.
It just sets up perfectly for preaching.

So I'm sure you've heard someone use a line like this on you
before: "Even though you know this story backward and forward,
I ask you to pay close attention to it again. Don't let your famil-
iarity with this passage blind you to what it has to say because its
message is simply too important to dismiss. Hang in there with
me just this one time, and let the story speak to you in a new way."

The testing of Jesus is a key passage for kingdom living. And
although you've probably read it a hundred times, chances are
you haven't read it today, in the midst of your current string of

circumstances, with your eyes perhaps more open than ever to your role in the kingdom and God's purpose for your life.

So sit back and listen.

There *will* be a test at the end.

In fact, you'll notice that I use the word *testing* rather than *temptation* in reference to this event in Jesus' life. Calling this a *temptation* is a little misleading, since Jesus was led into the wilderness "by the Spirit." This seems to imply that this test was inaugurated by his Father, who—according to the Scripture—cannot tempt us to evil (James 1:13).

What, then, was the purpose of this test? No doubt, the devil's purpose was to persuade Jesus to do wrong, to disobey his Father. But since Satan wasn't the one who started this, he couldn't be the one with the real purpose behind it. This testing was on God's initiative, and the issue was the Son's response to his messianic vocation. Was the Father wanting Jesus to prove his mettle, for the Son to show him that he had what it took to be the Messiah? Of course not. At Jesus' baptism, immediately prior to this forty-day period of testing, the Father had declared his divine approval of the Son. This test, then, had the purpose—the God-initiated purpose—of giving visible evidence to every creature that Jesus is King.

His test was for our benefit.

Some commentators compare this testing sequence with that of Adam's in the garden. Indeed, Jesus is the "last Adam" (1 Cor. 15:45), the one "who has been tested in every way as we are, yet without sin" (Heb. 4:15). But the primary context for understanding Christ's testing is found in Deuteronomy 6–8, where Israel faced a similar season of testing as they were poised to enter the promised land. In fact, all of the Old Testament references

Jesus quoted throughout this passage in response to the devil are found in this three-chapter section of Scripture. When the test came to Israel, of course, we know they failed badly. The Son of God, however—the true Israel, whom the Father had called out of Egypt (Matt. 2:15)—faced his time of testing and succeeded.

He was a perfect three-for-three.

TESTING GROUNDS

Before we dive headlong into this three-part story, however, let's start with this kingdom reality: *the devil is a real adversary.*

The devil had the most to lose by Jesus' inauguration of the kingdom of heaven, so it shouldn't surprise us that he would do his best to sidetrack God's Messiah. He always opposes kingdom activity, just as did in this scene from Jesus' life.

And he still loves to sidetrack us today. As Jesus said, "When anyone hears the word about the kingdom and doesn't understand it, the evil one comes and snatches away what was sown in his heart" (Matt. 13:19).

So be expecting him. He knows *who* you are and *where* you are. And he finds ridiculous joy in knocking you off center and turning your affections inward toward yourself. But be of good courage! One great lesson to learn from Jesus' testing is how God thwarts Satan's hostile intentions by using him to accomplish God's purposes in your life. Your loving and faithful Father has a reason for allowing Satan to test you: "so that the genuineness of your faith—more valuable than gold, which perishes though refined by fire—may result in praise, glory, and honor at the revelation of Jesus Christ" (1 Pet. 1:7). God has kingdom purposes for allowing his precious possessions to be tried in the fire—so that when you come through it, you shine for his glory. The kingdom of God cannot be deterred!

But this doesn't stop the devil from trying.

After Jesus had fasted forty days and nights in the wilderness—a reminder of the forty *years* Israel had spent in the wilderness (Deut. 8:2–3)—Satan came to him. (This is typical. He always approaches us when he thinks we're at our weakest.) His first temptation struck hard at Jesus' immediate needs: loneliness, hunger, and credibility.

All alone out here, Jesus? What kind of Father leaves his Son all by himself in the middle of nowhere with nothing to eat?

Hungry, Jesus? Surely for a miracle worker like you, these little loaf-sized stones are only bread in disguise.

You're the Son of God, Jesus? I might believe it myself if you'd prove it to me.

But Jesus responded by quoting a portion from this verse, Deuteronomy 8:3: "He humbled you by letting you go hungry; then He gave you manna to eat, which you and your fathers had not known, so that you might learn that man does not live on bread alone but on every word that comes from the mouth of the LORD."

Jesus knew what Israel had failed to comprehend—that we, God's people, can rely on the Father for our every need. But we have to put first things first.

Jesus' first desire was unquestioned obedience to the Father's plan for his life. Thus he would do nothing—absolutely nothing—that would compromise their relationship. This "first things first" reality is what Jesus would later teach his disciples, telling them to "seek first the kingdom" and trust God to provide all they needed (Matt. 6:33). When we tend first to our spiritual needs, God takes care of our physical needs without our even having to think about them.

That was test number one.

For his next act, the devil took Jesus to the pinnacle of the temple, whose main building (we know from historical research) was about 180 feet high. But when you take into account the topography of the area, Jesus' position at the top of the complex placed him some five hundred feet above the Kidron Valley. And Satan told him to hurl himself off. What a show Jesus would put on when the angels swooped down to catch him!

Once again the issue at stake was the Son's relationship to his Father. As Messiah, Jesus could expect God to protect him. But to pull a stunt like this—leaping from the temple roof—would be, in effect, putting God to the test. Would this be in keeping with the relationship the Father desired with him?

When we refuse to work but expect God to provide for us, we test God.

When we ignore the sound recommendations of our physician but expect God to keep us healthy, we test God.

When we disobey the direct word of God or the leading of his Holy Spirit but expect him to clean up our mess at the end, we test God.

Satan wanted to create an artificial crisis for the Son—for Jesus to place himself in a position where he could make demands on the Father's mercy. But the Son of God was called to live in a relationship where his trust demanded *no proof* on the Father's part.

And like the Son we can trust God to meet our needs in every situation that springs from our obedience, but not the ones we cause through our rebellion, selfishness, and neglect. That's testing God.

THE BIG QUESTION

Jesus' ordeal reached its climax in Satan's third and final test, a moment that brings us to the heart of the issue concerning the kingdom of God.

Jesus had to renounce the easy way to world authority, although he could possibly have argued that the ends justified the means. After all, the prophet Daniel had foreseen that the "son of man" would be given "authority to rule, and glory, and a kingdom; so that those of every people, nation, and language should serve Him" (Dan. 7:13–14). This was already in the books! Jesus knew he was on the path to fulfilling this prophecy, but he also knew it would come at the cost of much suffering and blood. Was Satan offering him the back door to the same prize? All Jesus had to do, it seemed, was worship Satan just this once—and save himself a lot of trouble.

But there are no shortcuts to kingdom greatness. The kingdom of God is always *glorious,* but it will not always be *glamorous.* We cannot share the glory without sharing the sufferings (1 Pet. 5:10).

So Jesus responded to Satan with firmness and finality. "You must worship the Lord your God, and you must serve Him only" (Matt. 4:10b). God had given this same warning to Israel in Deuteronomy 6:10–15, alerting them to avoid all other gods and to fear and worship the *living* God alone.

Israel failed this test. But Jesus remained steadfast. He knew that what Satan offered, his Father had already promised him—and had prepared the perfect way of getting there.

"Ask of Me, and I will make the nations Your inheritance and the ends of the earth Your possession" (Ps. 2:8). "All the ends of the earth will remember and turn to the LORD. All the families of the nations will bow down before You, for kingship belongs to the LORD; He rules over the nations" (Ps. 22:27–28). Notice again that God is moving all history toward his kingdom, that his eternal plan involves the ends of the earth—all nations and family groups. Hear the angel shout the news from the empty-tomb side of history: "The kingdom of the world has become the kingdom of our Lord and of His Messiah, and He will reign forever and ever!" (Rev. 11:15b).

How I love to be on the winning side!

We all face the same kind of tests Jesus did as he began his kingdom ministry:

1. *Putting physical needs first.* A quick glance at our checkbooks will confirm this. Where does our money go? How much of it do we spend on ourselves, and how much of it do we invest in eternal things, in God's kingdom work, in our children and others who are God's prized possessions on earth? Too often, all these things take a backseat to both our needs and our wants.

2. *Failing to trust God.* We often want God to prove himself to us before we launch out boldly into kingdom service. We want to have all the lines drawn in, all the money accounted for, all the organizational structure in place, all of our friends supportive and on board. But God simply asks us to trust him—to do things his way, at his initiative.

3. *Wanting temporary glory.* We face this final testing just about every day: "Will I live today for the kingdoms of the world and their glory, or will I live for the kingdom of God and my Father's reward?"

This is an issue I confront with regularity. I constantly have to ask myself, "Do I write books and fly across the country for speaking engagements because I desire men's glory or because I desire to advance the kingdom?"

I often observe good people pouring their energy and resources into pursuits that have no kingdom significance. These activities may produce a temporary level of success and acclaim, but what real difference does man's recognition make? Are the rewards of this world worth anything more than the air their words, plaques, and trophies displace?

The psalmist made his case for this with brutal honesty. "Do not be afraid when a man gets rich, when the wealth of his house increases. For when he dies, he will take nothing at all; his wealth will not follow him down. Though he praises himself during his lifetime—and people praise you when you do well for yourself—he will go to the generation of his fathers; they will never see the light. A man with valuable possessions but without understanding is like the animals that perish" (Ps. 49:16–20).

Everything we do must be measured by this litmus test: "Is it kingdom focused?"

Try a few test questions:

- Do I desire to be my best at work because my attitude and professionalism ultimately reflect on my heavenly Father?

- Do I seek to earn a good living so that I can meet the needs of my family and have excess from which to finance kingdom activity through my church and denomination?
- Do my lifestyle, calendar, and checkbook give clear testimony that I am seeking first the kingdom of God and my Father's approval?

In subsequent chapters we will discover that our responses to questions like these go to the heart of determining whether we're kingdom people, whether we're seeking the kingdoms of this world and their glory or the kingdom of God and our Father's reward, whether we're motivated by money and worldly fame or by eternal consequences and our Father's approval.

We find Jesus' ultimate response to this test in Matthew 4:17: "From then on Jesus began to preach, 'Repent, because the kingdom of heaven has come near!'" Jesus determined that he would join the Father in his kingdom activity.

May our passion be of a similar grade.

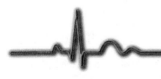

- Do you believe that the devil is real? Has he tested/tempted you? How? Did you yield to temptation or remain steadfast as a Christ follower?
- Have you ever placed physical needs ahead of spiritual needs? What happened?
- In your daily life, are you more often part of the kingdoms of the world or the kingdom of God?

Chapter 15

A KINGDOM INVASION

**When He saw the crowds, He went up on the mountain,
and after He sat down, His disciples came to Him.
Then He began to teach them.**

MATTHEW 5:1–2

THEY WERE YOUNG and energetic. They longed for action, adventure, achievement, and happiness. They had left their homes and put their careers on hold to follow a strong, compelling man who promised to make them "fishers of men" (see Matt. 4:18–22).

We know them, of course, by names like James and John, Peter and Andrew. Like most young Jewish men of their day, they felt a keen responsibility toward God and a certain pride in their nation. They lived at a time when the tyrannical military government of Rome occupied the land of Abraham, Isaac, and Jacob—a time when racial prejudice was prevalent and the staggering taxation policies of the empire had reduced many to poverty. These were hard years to be a Jewish citizen in Palestine.

In the midst of this darkness, several voices were crying out for reform:

- The zealots wanted to raise an army and fight for freedom. They believed that nothing short of political overthrow—regime change—would solve their problems.

- The Pharisees saw the solution in religious purity and separation, in strict and slavish obedience to the law.
- The Sadducees straddled the fence, wanting to maintain their heritage but worried about offending a world superpower.
- Some had even found a way to bargain with Rome. Their philosophy went something like, "If you can't change the situation, at least make money from it."

And into this cacophony of disparate chords—into this inescapable mix of depressingly bad news—came a single man, "preaching the good news of the kingdom" (Matt. 4:23).

Oh, how refreshing his message was!

How well Jesus knew that these were critical times he had entered in history—when nations were in conflict, when people felt controlled and confused by their leadership, when the only kingdoms they had ever experienced were bringing little more into their lives than distrust and corruption.

But was their situation all that different from the one we're in today? Do we not need a kingdom focus just as badly as they did?

Today we are witnessing the crumbling of standards we once considered sacred. The scourge of abortion! Crude sexuality that rivals that of Roman decadence, paraded into our national consciousness as normal behavior! Pandemic levels of disease arising from casual, free sex! An escalating divorce rate! Deep despair that has led to rampant drug abuse!

Like Christ's first-century hearers, we need to know about a kingdom that can change the hearts of men, that can make a real and lasting difference on earth and in eternity, that can invade our culture through ordinary people like us and "turn the hearts of

fathers to their children, and the disobedient to the understanding of the righteous, to make ready for the Lord a prepared
people" (Luke 1:17).

We need to hear Jesus tell us again: "Seek first the kingdom."

It's the only hope we have.

A KINGDOM APPEAL

Jesus declared his kingdom message most clearly in the three-
chapter section we now call the Sermon on the Mount (Matt.
5–7). In it he told the multitudes gathered around him that a new
kingdom was at work in the world—already! right now!—and
that those who would hear and respond to him and his word
could become immediate citizens by repenting of their sins and
following him.

Although entrance into this kingdom was as simple as turning
away from sin and turning toward him, Jesus wanted to make sure
they understood that life in his kingdom would not be easy. The
reward would be incomparable, yes, but the way would be hard.
Their righteousness would have to exceed that of the Pharisees—
was that even possible?—because his people's character would
give credibility to their kingdom citizenship and support their
claim of being sons and daughters of God.

They would be called upon to embody the character of their
Father in heaven.

This is why—again, because of the high standards of kingdom
living—it is so critical for you to confirm with the Lord that you
have indeed repented of your sins and received him as Savior
before trying to accomplish this kind of lifestyle.

These kingdom principles from the Sermon on the Mount are not for the unsaved. They are not (as many have interpreted them) a sort of ethical creed devoid of the person of Christ and his demands on our hearts. These ideals will challenge you in every area of your life and offer you incredible blessing as a result of God's mercy and your obedience—but they cannot save you.

Some people truly believe they can earn their way into heaven by obeying these teachings. But the pattern of obedience Jesus described is far more demanding than even the Old Testament law, which was in itself an impossible ethic. This, of course, was God's design—that his people would learn obedience but would also realize how far their abilities fell short, how much they needed his help and enabling.

Some deify the words themselves, reading the sermon with little concern for the One who gave it. People who embrace the social gospel, for example, see certain aspects of the Sermon on the Mount as a charter for world peace, if only all peoples and nations would take it to heart. Such a surface application ignores the radical nature of the beatitudes, which can only be performed by those with a transformed heart and Holy Spirit empowerment. Others see it as a wonderful ideal that would certainly make the world a better place to live, but they don't consider it realistic in the light of man's selfish nature.

We're going to spend a good deal of time focusing on this pivotal Bible passage, but I want to make sure we start with a solid understanding of what the Sermon on the Mount is—and what it is not!

It is not a plan of salvation. Or a humanistic plea for a kinder and gentler life ethic. Or an impractical demand for perfection. We do not have the luxury of listening in on this sermon just to enjoy its depth or beauty, for it is much more than that. It is not simply an excerpt of wise teaching to be compared and supplemented with the words and writings of other religious thinkers. *These are the words of God himself,* intended for those who have become kingdom citizens by grace. It sets out the demands which God's grace makes upon his people. It outlines the responsibilities of kingdom citizens.

This is teaching built on relationship.

And this is precisely what transforms these moral standards from being oppressive rules and regulations into being grace-filled guidelines for kingdom-invaded living!

Even believers in Christ can often make the mistake of thinking they must work their way into God's approval. Even those who have been forgiven of their sins can feel beaten down by years of inconsistency and failure. But no matter where you are in your Christian walk, the Sermon on the Mount—properly understood—offers the opportunity for you to experience kingdom blessings in present time. It is not too late. It is here and it is now.

We don't walk this kingdom path alone. We walk it with the King's arm around our shoulder. And therefore, he turns it into a pilgrimage of pure delight.

So let's sit down with the crowd and listen.

Our King is speaking.

A QUICK OVERVIEW

In the following few chapters, we're going to isolate several key verses from the Sermon of the Mount and see their vital importance for kingdom living. But before doing that, we need to look at the sermon as a whole because some big themes emerge when we view the big picture.

1. *A new definition of blessing.* The beatitudes (5:3–12) are the most recognized part of the Sermon on the Mount, serving as a powerful and engaging introduction. They redefine *blessing* to mean "those who have God as their king." This radically alters the view many of us have embraced or been taught. We have often thought of *blessing* in terms of material things, physical healing, or a parking place near the door. All of these things may be fine, but they live under the umbrella of the only blessing we really need: relationship with the King. Everything else is nice but nonessential.

2. *God's desire for the nations.* The salt and light declaration (5:13–16) reminds us of a theme that ran throughout our Old Testament study in previous chapters. God is still seeking people, families, churches, and denominations who will be both salt (embodying his name) and light (embracing his mission) in the world. God's kingdom purpose has not changed.

3. *The reason for righteousness.* If there is one key idea in the sermon, it is *righteousness.* Jesus used the term five times (5:6, 10, 30; 6:1, 33), teaching us that the main passion and priority of kingdom people is to showcase God's righteousness, to reveal the change his Holy Spirit can make in a person's life. The Pharisees' righteousness had shown itself to be artificial and external, based

on rigid legalism. It was all about *them*. Jesus taught a righteousness that would begin in our hearts and flow out through our character, a depth and quality of life that is all about *him*.

He makes this plain in Matthew 6:33: "Seek first the kingdom of God and His righteousness, and all these things will be provided for you." The passionate pursuit of righteousness, the act of submitting ourselves to God so that his holiness shines through us, is job one for the believer. Everything else just kind of falls into line after that.

This same idea resonates through the "surpassing righteousness" section (5:17–48), the six examples Jesus gives of how kingdom living intensifies and internalizes the Old Testament law. Instead of simply viewing these verses individually—as isolated teachings on anger, sexual impurity, divorce, dishonesty, revenge, and reactions to persecution—see them framed by the concluding verses of the fifth chapter. What is our one, defining reason for loving others, running from sexual sin, keeping our marriage vows, speaking the truth, turning the other cheek, and loving our enemies? "So that you may be sons of your Father in heaven," revealing his character.

The reason for going above and beyond in these and all other areas of life is to showcase our King. We don't begin by trying to master these kingdom principles through sheer willpower. We begin by wanting one thing—to display our Father's character to the world. And then, as the Holy Spirit takes control, these other things—love, purity, truth, freedom—just start to happen through us. When we "seek first the kingdom of God and His righteousness," he does the work of revealing his *own* righteousness through us. This is the only way it works.

4. *The desire for only one reward.* In Matthew 6:1–18, Jesus looked at the integrity of kingdom people and their singular desire for the reward of their Father. This passion impacts the way we practice our righteousness through activities such as prayer, fasting, and giving—not to please others, just to please our Father. Even the prayer of Jesus (6:9–13)—which forms a sort of centerpiece for the entire sermon—is taken up with seeking God's glory, not our own.

5. *A whole kingdom perspective.* Immediately following the prayer, Jesus discussed the priorities of kingdom people (6:19–34). Our lives are to focus on God's kingdom, not worrying about the details and demands of everyday life of our own little "kingdoms." Jesus also described the kinds of relationship skills available to the kingdom person (7:1–12)—the freedom to be genuine, to let God be the judge of people's hearts, to do for others what we would want done for us. He closed, then, with an appeal to total surrender, complete loyalty, and absolute trust in the King and his word (7:13–27).

THE INVASION OF GOD'S KINGDOM

Jesus' message was not like anything these early disciples had ever heard. Everyone was saying so: "When Jesus had finished this sermon, the crowds were astonished at His teaching. For He was teaching them like one who had authority, and not like their scribes" (7:28–29). He promised that God's rule and reign were invading planet Earth through his own ministry. A passion for his righteousness would penetrate their very lives, and they in turn would spread the news of this kingdom, becoming fishers of men. Jesus was not simply inviting them to become *recipients* of the kingdom. He was empowering them to become *agents* of the kingdom, giving them the joy of encouraging others to experience its full share of blessing, now and forever.

Yes, even this very day, God promises blessing—not to the strong, the powerful, and the mighty but to the poor in spirit, to those who mourn, who are gentle, who hunger for his righteousness, who are merciful and pure in heart, who seek peace even when it's returned as persecution.

And how does God bless them?

He declares, "The kingdom of heaven is theirs."

They shall be comforted. They shall inherit the earth, enjoying kingdom benefits even on this side of heaven. They shall be satisfied in their quest for righteousness. They shall be shown the indescribable mercy of being called the sons and daughters of God. They will not always be spared the sting of suffering, but they will receive the eternal reward of their Father.

As we move into the next section, we'll go inside the Sermon on the Mount, seeing more and more about what "His Kingdom Is."

But we are now at a point where we can begin to define who a *kingdom person* is:

1. Kingdom people are born of the Spirit.
2. They are passionate about righteousness, about demonstrating God's character.
3. They are continually aware of their Father's presence and pleased with his reward.
4. They understand that only a house built on the rock of God's Word will stand.

They enjoy the blessing of God, a constant relationship with the King of glory.

And isn't that blessing enough?

- In a movie or on the news, have you watched an invasion? Invasions seem to evoke different responses. How have you seen people respond in an invasion?
- Has anything in your life ever changed so rapidly that you could equate it with an invasion?
- Have you ever felt "blessed"?
- Do you think our country is "blessed"? Why/why not?
- Do you think that blessing will continue? Why/Why not?

SECTION 4

His Kingdom Is

Chapter 16

GETTING HUNGRY?

Blessed are those who hunger and thirst for righteousness, because they will be filled.

MATTHEW 5:6

I NEVER WAS A Rolling Stones fan, but I do remember their song that went, "I can't get no . . . satisfaction. I try and I try and I try and I try, but I can't get no . . . satisfaction." I feel almost silly writing these words on paper, but their lyrics are nearly without rival in capturing mankind's emptiness. This song—in its day—echoed the prevailing sentiments of a generation.

Has anything really changed over the years, though? We still see the many futile attempts people make—and we make—to find satisfaction. Bigger houses, better jobs, more money, faster cars, classier clothes, more outrageous and expensive thrills. These are all part of the quest to find satisfaction in life. We may call it fulfillment, happiness, or status, but we're all seeking to find meaning and purpose.

Satisfaction.

The miracle of the kingdom, though, is that when Jesus told us to pursue righteousness with abandon, to set our affections on him and his kingdom, he was actually offering us the only satisfaction life can give. In pursuing his kingdom, we discover that all the things we once considered worthy goals take a backseat to that of knowing God and experiencing the freedom that comes from his rule in our lives.

So do you want satisfaction? Then you want the kingdom because nothing else satisfies . . . though we try and we try and we try and we try.

SATISFACTION THROUGH BANKRUPTCY

It still seems odd to us, though, that Jesus instructed us to begin our pursuit of kingdom satisfaction by declaring ourselves spiritually bankrupt, "poor in spirit." I guess he wanted to show us right off the bat that this was to be a radical new way of living.

I've walked with people through the experience of *financial* bankruptcy, so I have an understanding sympathy for the humiliation it causes. *Spiritual* bankruptcy is a humbling experience, as well, but that's where the similarities end. For example, there's no guarantee in bankruptcy that the person will ever recover financially. Legal bankruptcy is sometimes little more than a brief delay in a person's total ruin. But Jesus promised that when we file for *spiritual* bankruptcy—when we recognize our complete inability to pay our debts or to dig ourselves out of the hole—the "kingdom of heaven" is ours (Matt. 5:3).

We can bank on it.

But to enjoy the satisfaction Jesus offers, we need to know what being "poor in spirit" is. *It is the emptying of ourselves before God, humbly acknowledging our impoverished spiritual condition.*

The more we recognize the absolute nature of our spiritual need, the more we will seek the reign of God in our lives. The less attached we are to this world, the more passionate we will become about the kingdom.

Matthew gave us a vivid example of what it means to be poor in spirit. He told of a centurion who came to Jesus on behalf of his paralyzed servant (Matt. 8:5–13). Jesus immediately replied, "I will come and heal him." But the Roman officer didn't dare ask Jesus to come to his home. "'Lord,' the centurion replied, 'I am not worthy to have You come under my roof. But only say the word, and my servant will be cured.'" *His sense of unworthiness was a kingdom response.*

We struggle with this poor-in-spirit beatitude because our world places such an exaggerated emphasis on self-reliance and self-confidence. We want to give the impression that we've got it all together. We've been led to believe that if we get enough education, lose enough weight, firm up, straighten up, and develop a positive mental attitude, we will be happy.

But we have swallowed a lie that has left us empty. The gospel of the kingdom says that we must first declare spiritual bankruptcy in order to know real satisfaction.

And because this is God's Word—because this promise of Jesus is absolute, unchanging truth—that's why the poor in spirit are always the first to recognize the surpassing value of the kingdom. They are the ones who understand that this "treasure," this "priceless pearl," is worth liquidating everything (Matt. 13:44–46). They are the ones who are not ashamed to "become like children" in order to "enter the kingdom of heaven" (Matt. 18:3). They are the least, and yet they are "the greatest in the kingdom" (Matt. 18:4).

They have nothing but God, but they have all they want.

They are satisfied.

And we should long to be counted among their number.

Satisfaction through Mourning

Here's another unexpected secret of satisfaction: "Blessed are those who mourn, because they will be comforted" (Matt. 5:4).

Kingdom mourning is not some kind of morbid depression. It is simply the natural response to our own spiritual bankruptcy. It is the result of seeing God in his absolute holiness and seeing our own sinfulness in stark contrast. When confronted with God's purity, "those who mourn" are utterly stricken by the enormity of debt they owe.

This is the mourning of Isaiah, after seeing "the Lord seated on a high and lofty throne," angels encircling the room, the very foundation quaking beneath his feet, the whole temple filling with the smoke of God's glory. And without stopping for thought or explanation, Isaiah blurts out the only thing his soul knows to say: "Woe is me, for I am ruined, because I am a man of unclean lips and live among a people of unclean lips, and because my eyes have seen the King, the Lord of Hosts" (Isa. 6:1, 5).

This was the experience of Paul, who cried out concerning his ongoing struggle with sin, "What a wretched man I am! Who will rescue me from this body of death?" (Rom. 7:24).

It is the experience of every kingdom citizen.

But—good news!—those who mourn over their sin are "comforted" by the knowledge of their forgiveness. So while our awareness of need is continual and never departs from us, *God's comfort* is also continual. Our tears are tears of joy.

We hurt, but we are satisfied.

This is more than a *personal* mourning, though. It's also a *shared* mourning—a sadness not only over our own sin but also over the damaging effects of sin in our world, in our churches, in our extended families, among our friends. Kingdom citizens understand that sin is the bitter result of Satan's deception, whose goal is to steal and kill and destroy and whose success rate is astounding . . . and showing no signs of letting up.

It should not surprise us, then, that we even find Jesus weeping—weeping over the sin of Jerusalem (Luke 13:34), weeping at the grave of Lazarus (John 11:35). When he wept at Lazarus's tomb, it was not so much for the death of his friend. After all, Jesus was minutes away from bringing him back to life! No, Jesus' grief was over the horrid, ugly, foul thing we call "sin" that had introduced death into life to begin with.

Several years ago we visited a popular resort beach with our young children. I was shocked by the overt sexuality, bordering on pornography, on display in virtually every shop. Many of the young people who staggered down the boardwalk had a vacant look in their eyes that appalled us. Our entire family was anxious to leave. As we drove away, I remember all of us having a great sense of sadness. We were grieving over sin and its disastrous impact on those who seek satisfaction from it . . . and come up so predictably empty.

Those who have become part of the kingdom family will always mourn over sin—both *our* sin and *others'* sin. We recognize this as the work of the adversary, whose short-lived but cruel kingdom is tottering under the onslaught of *God's* kingdom. But for us, the sorrowing poor, our tears are turned into happy laughter through the intervention of the Messiah, whose kingdom pleasure is to "comfort all who mourn" (Isa. 61:2).

SATISFACTION THROUGH MEEKNESS

Jesus said the "meek," the "gentle," would "inherit the earth" (Matt. 5:5). But our culture has created a different breed of inheritors. There is nothing remotely meek about the heroes of our day. Meekness and gentleness are not virtues we greatly admire, and therefore this beatitude may not appeal to us.

In our minds meekness is often associated with weakness, passivity, or even cowardice. Or we may think it's simply a person's natural disposition, a tendency to be quiet and mellow, which some have and some don't. If either of these two is correct, (1) Jesus wouldn't have praised it, and (2) those of us who aren't so calm and collected by nature would be out of luck in satisfying Christ's command.

The Bible says that "gentleness" is a fruit of the Spirit (Gal. 5:23)—a Christlike character trait which is produced in the believer's life by the Holy Spirit, not by natural birth. And furthermore, meekness is not weakness. "In the ancient world, meekness connoted power that was bridled by gentleness. That is why the ancient Greeks did not say 'meek as a mouse' but 'meek as a lion.'"[1]

Power, restrained by gentleness. I like that.

In Numbers 12:3 we're told that Moses was the meekest man in the world. But think back: Here's a man who faced down Pharaoh and led Israel to the promised land. You'd think he'd deserve a little more respect than being tagged with the "meekness" label! In the context of Numbers 12, however, Moses was facing a situation where his brother and sister were challenging his leadership, casting aspersions on his character, and threatening his reputation. How do you think this man who stamped his staff at Pharaoh's feet, demanding that he *let these people go,* would respond to these two who were questioning his ability to lead? Apparently, he said nothing. Is that what we would have done? And when *God* responded by striking Miriam white with leprosy, Moses cried out to the Lord for her healing. Is that the first thought we would have had?

Yes, Moses was meek. He possessed power under control.

We see this quality throughout the ministry of Jesus:

In the wilderness testing. Satan offered him everything a man could want. And Jesus could have had it all—physical satisfaction, public acclaim, universal power. But he chose to remain in submission to his Father.

In the Garden of Gethsemane. His human flesh begged to avoid the cross, but he submitted to the Father's eternal plan, "not what I will, but what You will" (Mark 14:36).

On the cross. Here we see the supreme example of power under control. Do you remember the taunting cry of the criminal? "Aren't You the Messiah? Save Yourself and us!" (Luke 23:39). Everything in Jesus' human nature must have desired to come down and show them the fierce anger of the Lord. If we were there, we would have *cheered* if he had torn himself free of the cross and taken his own revenge. But it was his meekness that held him there, enabling him to endure the shame and buy mankind's redemption.

What about us?

Let's illustrate meekness this way, and see how strong it is: The Pharisees avoided adultery because of external pressure because of reputation. Sometimes that's about the only thing that keeps *us* in line, as well. But what if all restraints were somehow removed? What if we were absolutely certain that no one would know? Even in that kind of tempting situation, meekness would enable us to choose not to take advantage of an evil opportunity. Meekness would remind us that we embody God's name. Meekness would help us keep his kingdom purposes in mind.

The meek get it all, a taste of heaven while inheriting the earth. They are surrendered so completely to God that they have become his instrument of blessing to others. God works through them to accomplish his will and advance his kingdom. They don't glory in themselves or demand their own rights. Instead, they leave everything—their lives, their rights, and their futures—in the capable hands of God.

Meekness defines the extent of our surrender . . . and the extent of our satisfaction.

SATISFACTION THROUGH HUNGER

One more. The words "hunger and thirst" (Matt. 5:6) suggest a deep, profound, even painful desire that increases to the point of desperation until it is fed.

That's how the kingdom citizen pursues righteousness—like a hungry man starving for supper, like a woman thirsty after an outdoor run—with an appetite that's getting more directed and ferocious all the time.

Our hunger for righteousness should be like that—both recurring and ongoing. When we eat a sandwich at lunch, for example, it may hold us for a while, but it doesn't satisfy our hunger for the rest of our lives. As long as we're growing as Christians, our appetite for righteousness should always keep growing. When we lose our appetite for the Lord and his kingdom, when we're just as content with the world's junk food as we are with the Word of God, that's when we know something is wrong.

Here's what kingdom hunger is like:

1. It is a hunger for *God*, an unquenchable desire to know him.
2. It is a desire to be free from *sin* because sin separates us from God.
3. It is a desire to be free from the *power* of sin and controlled by God's Spirit.
4. It is a desire to be free from the *desire* for sin and eager to please the Father.
5. It is a desire to be like *Jesus*.

How, then, do we seek righteousness?

We let God show us who we really are. We do away with the entire pretense of human righteousness. As long as we think we're better than most, we are not hungry for righteousness. Spiritual fulfillment, like all the other blessings of the beatitudes, begins with an awareness of our spiritual bankruptcy.

We let sin and kingdom substitutes go. This is not easy to do because we've grown so accustomed to having these things around. But to seek righteousness, we must actively avoid all unrighteousness. We must also spot and remove anything that tends to dull our spiritual appetite, whether it's overtly sinful or not. It might be NFL football, or boating, or a perfectly harmless hobby. But if it gets in the way of our pursuit of righteousness, it needs to go. Our kingdom hunger demands it.

I'm telling you, this requires real sacrifice. But it results in real satisfaction because those who orient their "hunger and thirst" in the direction of righteousness are guaranteed to find themselves "filled." When was the last time any *sin* left you feeling that way?

Spiritual bankruptcy. Spiritual mourning. Spiritual gentleness. Spiritual hunger.

These are the only pathways to spiritual satisfaction.

 *Less money is being saved or contributed to churches and charitable organizations, and more is being spent on credit card interest, recreation, alcohol, gambling (primarily through state lotteries) and pets.* (Source: Baptist Press)

- What evidence do you see that few people today are satisfied?
- Think of people you know who seem satisfied. Do they have any of the things society seems to say are essential to success—wealth, fame, power? If not, why do you think they are content?
- How would your life have to change for you to find spiritual satisfaction?

Chapter 17

A NEW TAKE-OUT MENU

Blessed are the merciful, because they will be shown mercy.

MATTHEW 5:7

I'VE HEARD THAT OUR BEHAVIOR in rush hour traffic is a fairly good indicator of our personality. One driver, for example, can be laid back, listening to his music and enjoying his time in the car, while another driver has a death lock on the steering wheel. His horn is blaring, and his face is flushed from the rush of adrenaline. To him the drive home is a competitive event.

With this idea in mind, let's pose a familiar scene and see how you'd react: You are virtually parked on the interstate, waiting somewhat patiently in a line of traffic that's moving at a snail's pace for as far as you can see. In the rearview mirror you spot a car cruising down the shoulder of the road, merrily passing scores of other commuters. And just before the driver's self-made express lane disappears, he arrives beside you smiling and waving. He wants you to let him slip back into traffic in front of you.

How do you respond?

"Park it, turkey! Your tires will rot off before I budge an inch!" Your sense of justice would prompt you to be both judge and jury. You're not being deliberately ugly, but you've been provoked! I mean, if you knew this individual had a legitimate *reason* to be

in such a hurry—like having a sick child in the car, for example— you would gladly give way. In that case your sense of justice would prompt a different response.

But mercy is quite difference from justice. Mercy does not depend on circumstances and contexts. It *exceeds* justice. Before it judges, it seeks to understand. Instead of *ending* in empathy (if the person has a good enough excuse), mercy *begins* with empathy, the ability to identify. It then progresses into forgiveness and finds its culmination when we joyfully give what is undeserved.

I'll admit, this is radical. Kingdom living requires us to order from a whole new menu of behavior options, not the same old fare as the rest of the world. This is turn-the-other-cheek stuff. It's about taking Christlike traits out into our world and workplaces, into our homes and churches, even into our cars on a rainy after- noon at rush hour.

Kingdom living changes everything.

In the last chapter we looked at the first four beatitudes, which primarily describe who a kingdom person is supposed to *be*— humble, repentant, hungry, under control. These next four, how- ever, describe what a kingdom person is supposed to *do,* the way we are designed to relate to others—with mercy and peace, with pure motives and patience.

This progression of thought—from being to doing—brings us to an important point: *Kingdom character precedes action. Holiness precedes mission.*

- A Christian *is* something before he *does* something.
- We are not meant to *control* our Christianity; it is meant to control *us.*

- We don't behave mercifully just because it's the Christian thing to do; we respond with mercy because we are Christians.

In other words, our behavior is fruit and not effort. We don't merely apply these kingdom characteristics onto the surface of our lives, like expensive veneer glued to cheap wood. They are crafted instead at the core of our being. They are like fine, solid hardwood, handmade by the Spirit of God, and ready to be taken out and shown to the world—for the glory of our Maker.

A SIDE OF MERCY

Before we look carefully at mercy, we must first make a clear disclaimer. Mercy is not an easygoing, open-minded, wishy-washy attitude that winks at sin. Our postmodern culture has embraced the idea of tolerance to argue that everyone has the right to do whatever he wants. And because *mercy* and *tolerance* are such close cousins in our world's way of thinking, the two terms have become almost interchangeable.

But biblical *mercy* and *tolerance* are not the same thing. God is merciful, but he is not tolerant. He doesn't let sin slip by unnoticed or unpunished. Some people have a hard time understanding this. They believe the gospel message itself is a picture of God's tolerance. But it is not. God hasn't overlooked our sin; he has merely arranged payment for it through the blood of Christ.

So mercy, we see, is more powerful than tolerance. Tolerance costs its giver nothing. But mercy will always cost its giver something, perhaps even everything.

Mercy is also not the same as *pity*. In Jesus' parable of the Good Samaritan, for example, the priest and the Levite probably felt sorry for the man who had been beat up by the robbers and left for dead. But only the Samaritan moved beyond feeling and emotion into merciful action.

Perhaps the clearest example of biblical mercy comes from Matthew 20:1–16, where Jesus compared the kingdom of heaven to a landowner who went out early in the morning to hire laborers for his vineyard. You'll remember that he offered each of them standard pay for a day's work, and they apparently all seemed fine with the arrangement. Then when the owner returned to the marketplace at various times throughout the day and saw other potential workers standing idle, he hired additional men as well. These workers probably assumed they would earn some sort of prorated amount since the landowner simply told them he would pay them "whatever is right." The *final* group of laborers, in fact— not hired until the eleventh hour—would barely have had time even to *get* to the workplace, much less put any work in before night fell and the workers came in to collect their pay.

You'll recall what happened then. The landowner instructed the foreman to start paying the men, beginning with the last group first. And to everyone's surprise, this bunch received a full day's wage! For less than an hour's work!

No doubt, these men were overwhelmed at the owner's generosity—but hardly as overwhelmed as the *first* group, who were flabbergasted to find that they, too, would be receiving merely a day's wage for their efforts. They immediately cried foul—no fair!—even though they were given exactly the amount they had been promised. The owner rebuked them for being jealous over his generosity. "Don't I have the right to do what I want with my business? Are you jealous because I'm generous?" (v. 15).

God is like that—never doing less than he promised and pouring on the mercy besides. No one in this story was treated unfairly. Even the gift of a day's work was an act of mercy.

His gifts to us are like that, too—not earned by our deeds but distributed by his grace. This is why he expects his people to show mercy to others—in order to show forth his character. We can be merciful because we ourselves have received his mercy (Matt. 5:7).

Anytime we find ourselves thinking, "They got what they deserved," or, "They just don't deserve that," we're thinking in terms of justice, not mercy. We're reading from the wrong take-out menu. The kingdom calls us to identify with the needs of those around us, respond in compassion, and seek to give more than they deserve.

A SIDE OF PURITY

"Blessed are the pure in heart" (Matt. 5:8).

Our culture doesn't provide us an easy environment for maintaining purity of heart. But is it any wonder that our *world* is confused about standards of purity, when the modern-day *church* seems to be sending out such mixed signals about it? It's not hard to think of some recent examples and observations:

- Several denominations have suggested that "responsible cohabitation" should be seen as a recognized option to marriage.
- Other denominations have split or are at the point of splitting over the issue of homosexuality.
- Meanwhile, many studies indicate that teenagers who claim to be Christians are as sexually active as their *non-*Christian classmates.

- Furthermore, the dress, language, and lifestyle of many believers today more clearly reflect the norms of the culture than the character of their Father.

The "pure in heart" are few and far between.

And this must break the heart of God.

Many people who address this subject deal only with the symptoms, not the cure. It's true that part of our job as kingdom people is to expose the moral failures of our day. According to Galatians 5:21, "Those who practice such things will not inherit the kingdom of God." So this is serious, and it should cause us to "mourn" over the sins of our society.

But purity of heart refers to more than the avoidance of sinful behaviors. It is instead a *singleness of mind and purpose.* The reason the "pure in heart" are able to be that way is not because they have more self-control than others but because they have only one master, only one King. They don't have conflicting loyalties.

The Scripture comes down hard on the divided heart. It says, for example, that serving both God and money is worse than serving money alone because the divided heart pulls us in two directions. Being lukewarm (to quote another biblical reference) is worse than being either cold or hot. Better to be cold, the Bible says, than to be a tasteless, repulsive, lukewarm drink that's trying to be both hot and cold at the same time.

All of our behaviors come from the "overflow of the heart" (Matt. 12:34). So when our hearts are pure and undivided, kind words and responsible actions just naturally flow out through our lives. That's why the gospel is about the *heart* of man, about being cleansed from sin and given a new nature, a new heart that desires to be holy "as the One who called you is holy" (1 Pet. 1:15).

Our problem is not our environment or our parents. It is the purity of our hearts. Adam lived in a perfect environment, and he had God himself for a parent, but he still sinned . . . because his heart was divided.

The kingdom citizen has chosen the kingdom of God over the kingdoms of the world, and this choice has created a singleness of purpose. As a result, Jesus said the "pure in heart" are able to "see God"—to recognize his work amid everyday events—healing marriages, granting his people favor, giving us strength in the midst of grief, protecting us from harm and evil, providing opportunities to be merciful to others. Purity of heart enables us to see kingdom activity all day—every day—because our hearts are tuned in to one single frequency. We're ordering off the same page.

A SIDE OF PEACE

Another kingdom characteristic is peace. I'm not talking about being "peaceniks" or "peace lovers" but being "peace-makers" (Matt. 5:9).

God is the supreme example of this. Paul marveled at how God had reconciled two irreconcilable groups into one kingdom community, tearing down the "dividing wall of hostility" that separated Jews and Gentiles and making "both groups one" through the blood of Christ. "He is our peace," Paul said (Eph. 2:14)—the one who brings enemies together as friends in the kingdom of God.

And because this is the character of our Father, peacemaking should be a mark of kingdom people, as well. We are to be active and persistent in our efforts to resolve conflicts, restore relationships, and repair broken walls. We must refuse to retaliate when wronged (Matt. 5:39) but love our enemies (Matt. 5:44), even to the point of genuinely praying for the good of those who persecute and belittle us.

Paul gives clear directions for the peacemaker in Romans 12:17–21. We should:

1. Never pay back "evil for evil."
2. Do what is "honorable in everyone's eyes."
3. Make every effort to "live at peace with everyone."
4. Refuse to "avenge ourselves" when harmed or threatened.
5. Instead, we should "conquer evil with good."

As a result, we will so resemble our Father that others will know us as the "sons of God."

No other kingdom activity bears a more powerful witness to the Father's character than this commitment to peacemaking. That's why when we're estranged from someone in our family or church, when we've given up seeking peace and reconciliation, our hearts will tell us that we're choking the character of the Father within us.

Again, this is not easy. This is radical living. And I know there are certain dynamics and relationships—abusive situations, for example—where our peacemaking should not be naïve or even entered into at all without much prayer and outside assistance. But our hearts should never stop seeking peace and doing everything we can to be used of God, to advance his kingdom purposes.

A SIDE OF BLESSING

Truly, kingdom living in a fallen world is radical by definition. As kingdom citizens, we recognize our own spiritual poverty, mourn over our sinfulness, and place ourselves at God's full and complete disposal. Out of this self-emptying comes an insatiable appetite for righteousness, which God fills with his power and supernatural blessing. What emerges through us, then, is a new and radical lifestyle. We go beyond the demands of justice to treat people with mercy. We are pure in motive and action. We commit ourselves to unity and reconciliation in all our relationships.

But perhaps the biggest thing that causes us to pull back from going all the way into kingdom living is this: the world cannot ignore us if we do. If we commit ourselves to the kingdom, people may love us, but they also may hate us. If the example of Jesus is any indication—*and it is!*—the world's response to us will often be scorn, sarcasm, and stinging insult.

So kingdom living is a big responsibility and a genuine risk. We present to others an entirely different way of thinking and responding. We don't do business by the world's standards. We're not motivated by greed, position, power, or impurity. We don't go with the flow.

In short, we confront others every day with the kingdom of God on earth.

And the backlash is not always a pretty picture.

The student who is ostracized from her peer group because she refuses to drink or compromise her sexual purity knows what it means to be "persecuted for righteousness." The businessman who loses a large contract because he refuses to "play the game" and offer under-the-table amenities knows persecution. The parent who puts her family first when others at work or in her circle of friends are demanding unreasonable amounts of time and commitment may experience persecution.

And the Scripture tells us we're supposed to consider ourselves "blessed" because of this.

Don't be misled. Jesus was not suggesting that we should go out of our way to be persecuted. We're not to develop a martyr complex. Some Christians are so in-your-face with their faith, they alienate the unbeliever and receive harsh treatment in return. They're proud of being persecuted.

But kingdom righteousness—unlike *self*-righteousness—is Christlike, never showy or obnoxious. We're trying to display *Christ* to the unbeliever, not prove that we are right and superior. In serving our King, we should be prepared for potential insults and persecution. We shouldn't seek it, but it shouldn't surprise us either.

I hope you don't think this is a negative way to conclude our look at the beatitudes—a series of statements that each begin with the word "blessed" or "happy." Jesus promised that those who are persecuted receive "the kingdom of heaven" in return (Matt. 5:10). So this is a good thing. It's not a contradiction to say that the beatitudes describe both a life of happiness *and* a life that is unique, and different, and daily confronts others with the kingdom of God. It requires us to practice righteousness at any cost and then trust God to reward us.

I can promise you, nothing is quite as exhilarating as a kingdom lifestyle. As a kingdom person, you're free to stop defending yourself, retaliating, and harboring resentment. You're empowered to show mercy, live with purity of purpose, and serve as a peacemaker.

You're allowed to take life into your world.

- How is mercy evident in your relationships? How can you improve this kingdom quality?
- Is purity a desirable quality today? How pure is your life? How does this quality affect relationships?
- Is there an area of your life where you could improve relationships by becoming a peacemaker? What will you do?
- Have you ever been persecuted because you were a Christ follower? What happened? How did you respond? Was remaining faithful worth the cost?

Chapter 18

POINTS OF CONTACT

You are the salt of the earth. . . . You are the light of the world.

MATTHEW 5:13–14

IN THE LAST TWO CHAPTERS, we've covered a lot of kingdom ground. I hope you've been able to sense—and already know from experience—that the blessing of being in continual, vibrant relationship with the Father melts all of the responsibilities of kingdom living into privilege. He gives *so* much more in return, surrounds us in pure satisfaction, and promises even more to come in eternity. When we look at it on balance, we can hardly call it a sacrifice. Our Lord makes kingdom living one deep blessing after another.

But if these Sermon on the Mount demands still seem too high, their expectations too lofty, their standards too impractical and idealistic, imagine how they sounded to the raw, wet-behind-the-ears recruits who first heard Jesus' radical words? Without having the advantage—as we do—of knowing how Christ's life would play out and our salvation would be won, they were told by him to be poor in spirit, broken over their sin, meek, hungry for righteousness, merciful, pure in heart, peacemakers, and—on top of it all—to expect persecution in return. Yet, he said, this new lifestyle would make them happy—"blessed" beyond comprehension.

It must have been hard to believe.

Perhaps this is why, as Jesus continued his sermon, he brought his teachings even more clearly down to earth, talking about simple things they could more easily see and understand.

This kingdom of his was not going to be out of reach, lost in intangible ideas, a radical movement that was nothing more than a new way of thinking. Jesus needed his followers' feet to be on the ground, their changed lives visible in the eyes of their families and communities, their difference noticeable, their example observable, their witness real.

As real as salt. And light.

"YOU ARE THE SALT OF THE EARTH"

Salt, to us, is simply a condiment that enriches the flavor of food. But salt had many other uses in Jesus' day. Therefore, when he described his followers as being the "salt of the earth" (Matt. 5:13), he certainly triggered several different thoughts in the minds of his hearers.

1. *Salt was a preservative.* Before the days of refrigerators, people used salt to keep meat fresh, the way ham is still cured today. Salt, then, was an absolute essential to the people of Jesus' time, particularly in places where the fishing industry was the lifeblood of communities. Without salt, how could the fish be preserved long enough to get it to the marketplace? One of the well-known towns of ancient eastern Galilee, in fact, was named Taricheae, which actually meant "saltings," a reference to the salted fish industry that thrived there.

So in being described as "salt," Jesus' disciples knew he was challenging them to act like a preservative in the midst of a decaying world.

If you want to know why we're witnessing so much moral rottenness in our society, we can't blame it purely on the pagans. We must also conclude that our culture needs more salt—and that those of us who truly *are* the "salt of the earth" haven't been applying ourselves in the schools and neighborhoods and places of government where God has given us opportunities of influence. Our culture needs us. People's souls are dying in the midst of this decay, and we cannot simply run away from them and keep our salt to ourselves. This is a kingdom commission.

2. *Salt was an antiseptic.* Perhaps you've discovered this function of salt when you've waded into the ocean with an open cut. Salt is indeed a hearty disinfectant. But—as we know from this experience—a person's first exposure to the healing, germ-fighting qualities of salt is an initial sense of pain or discomfort. We need to remember this. People will many times not understand or applaud our desires to help cleanse them from the effects of sin through the "salt" of the gospel. They may plead for us to be more tolerant and understanding, or they may accuse us of being judgmental. But we are called to disinfect a dying world, and this means we cannot compromise with sin. We must love people enough to be honest with them, even if it hurts them . . . and us.

3. *Salt was also a catalyst for fire.* In Palestine an outdoor oven was called "earth," and one of the common fuels used for firing it was dried dung. (I'm serious.) To make the ovens burn better, people lined the bottom with salt plates and also sprinkled salt on the manure itself. Over time, however, the resultant chemical

reaction would cause the salt to lose its ability to perform this function well. By then the salt was useless, and it had to be discarded. This is why, in Luke 14:34–35, Jesus said that when salt had lost its salinity, it was no longer fit for either the earth (the oven) or the dung hill (the fuel).[1] The first followers of Jesus knew exactly what he was talking about. He was calling them to ignite spiritual fires on the earth, to be a helpful source of blessing in people's everyday lives.

WHO NEEDS THE SALT?

From these insights we can see that Jesus was speaking of salt to mean many different things. We, of course, primarily think of salt as a seasoning, as a flavor enhancer that brings out the taste of food. And this, too, is a key aspect of our "salty" kingdom calling. Christians are to be the spice of life. Our kingdom lifestyle should exude such a flavor that it creates in others a hunger and thirst for the gospel.

All of us have experienced firsthand the incredible thirst salt can create. My wife once made the mistake of leaving me as the babysitter for our miniature pinscher. One day when I was returning home, I discovered that this twelve-pound dog had somehow gotten into the cupboard and consumed an entire package of salt-cured country ham! He kept me awake that whole night, scratching at the door to be let out. I couldn't imagine why he needed out so often. But as I happened to glance out the window during one of his nocturnal wanderings, I couldn't believe my eyes! That little dog had his head buried in our fishpond. He was parched from the salt.

As Christians, we are to live in such a manner that the world is made thirsty for the gospel. The church of today has a tendency to brag about the size of our *saltshakers* (our church buildings) or the amount of salt we can put *into* our shakers (our worship attendance), rather than truly salting down our communities with the good news of Jesus Christ.

To be the "salt of the earth," we must embrace a lifestyle that is consistent with the character of our Father. It means we must take seriously the everyday demands of the beatitudes—not simply to receive personal and spiritual satisfaction from them, but to be an agent of healing, health, and wholeness to people in our world.

And to do this, we have to stay salty. Fresh. Alive. Hungry. Thirsty.

We cannot be like the ancient children of Israel, called by God to make a name for himself but profaning his name instead through their unwillingness to be radically obedient to him, to remain robust, to stay salty.

Neither can we be like the salt that lies dormant around the Dead Sea even today. It was once employed as a natural resource but is now so impure and tasteless that no one bothers to mine from its beds anymore.

Savorless Christianity is not a proud badge of religious purity but a clear sign of flavorless salt—unwanted, undesirable, uninviting. If our witness is going to have any credibility, if we're going to maintain good points of contact with others—and point them to Christ—we need to open our eyes to the needs around us.

And pour on the salt.

"You Are the Light of the World"

The storm clouds of death and darkness arrive more quickly in John's Gospel than in any of the others. By as early as chapter 7, some of Jesus' would-be disciples have already deserted him, and the plots against his life have already begun. It was into the smoke and mist of this gathering gloom that Jesus declared, "I am the light of the world. Anyone who follows Me will never walk in the darkness, but will have the light of life" (John 8:12).

Let this promise sink in. Christ has enabled us to escape the darkness of sin. He has given us himself—the "light of life." More than that, this One who is the "light of the world" has also made *us* "the light of the world" (Matt. 5:14). His Word declares it.

Truly his plan for lighting a dark world is to reveal himself through us.

This is why Paul encouraged the Philippian believers to be obedient, to serve the Lord and one another without grumbling and disputing, "so that you may be blameless and pure, children of God who are faultless in a crooked and perverted generation, among whom you shine like stars in the world" (Phil. 2:15). Our conduct—our saltiness—is the fuel that makes our witness—our light—stand out in the darkness.

We must not miss this connection between salt and light, between obedience and witness.

I have overheard Christians say that they choose to witness only through their lifestyle. In other words, they don't see any need to share a verbal witness of Christ's love with a lost neighbor. Please understand me. I believe a big part of living in the kingdom of God is about building relationships with others—

having them over to dinner, meeting them for coffee, letting them see Christ through the way we carry ourselves. But this idea that we shouldn't feel compelled to bring up his name as being the explanation for our Christian character is born from either unbelievable arrogance or incredible naivety.

We shouldn't be all salt and no light.

Jesus himself was always quick to explain, when others observed him and his lifestyle, that they were actually seeing the Father. And if Jesus, whose life was nothing short of salty perfection, chose to point out verbally to others that his obedience was a reflection of his Father's nature and kingdom, what makes us think we can do any less? We will only be effective Christian witnesses when we combine both life and word.

When someone sees your righteous lifestyle and asks you why you are different, how do you respond? Do you mumble out, "Oh, I'm just that kind of person"? No, you're not! You and I are nothing special. We are just like the world . . . except for one thing: the Holy Spirit indwells us, producing the life of Christ in us.

So *tell* them why you are different. You don't have to be offensive or confrontational about it when you give your personal testimony and share a simple plan of salvation. *Every kingdom citizen should know how to share his faith.* Some people may be more effective and gifted at this than others, but we are each called to illuminate the reasons behind our lifestyle, to use our salt to empower our light.

WHO NEEDS THE LIGHT?

Jesus used two different pictures to talk about the visibility of light.

1. *A single light on a lampstand.* This is an individual light, like the one on your bedside table, which Jesus said must be displayed and not hidden. Kingdom people may feel shy and tempted by Satan to keep their witness quiet for whatever reason—guilt, bad timing, intellectual inferiority. He's good at making us fearful of talking with others about Christ. He can make us feel so awkward and unworthy. But we should not be embarrassed to give testimony to our faith. We do it for the King and for his kingdom.

2. *The lights of the city on a hill.* This suggests the collective impact of having several lights gathered in one place. If you've ever been to a candlelight service, you've seen what happens when a single candle spreads its light to hundreds of others. Soon the entire room blazes with light. This image speaks to our need for Christian fellowship. When we join our light with the light of other believers, we become that city set on a hill.

I'm always surprised when I encounter people who claim to be children of the King but who have no desire to relate to other Christians, who don't feel any need for corporate worship and Bible study, who don't want to join their light with other believers—with fellow citizens of the realm—so their communities can be lit with the gospel. They may understand many things, but they don't understand the kingdom.

Jesus didn't say we *possess* the qualities of salt and light. He said, *we are* "the salt of the earth"! *We are* "the light of the world"! These are truth claims, not options. We are both salt and light by nature and by command. These affirmations of our kingdom calling are key ingredients in our passion to *embrace* his mission, *embody* his name, and *obey* his Word.

God set Israel among the nations so their light would draw men to him. And now that the kingdom of God has invaded the earth through the person of Jesus Christ, the Father wants to reveal himself through *us*—those who have been born into the kingdom by spiritual birth. Just as our salt is intended to create a thirst for Christ in the hearts of others, our light is also meant not to bring attention to us but to "give glory" to our Father in heaven, to draw the world to our King.

It doesn't really take all that much. A pinch of salt can go a long way, and even a tiny flashlight can flood a room with light. Your life and witness have enormous potential. They are your points of kingdom contact with the world.

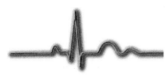

- Who has been salt in your life? How?
- Think of someone who draws people to them. What characteristics do they have that attract people? Do they reflect "the light of the world"?
- Are you an active part of a community of believers? How does that affect your light and your lifestyle?

Chapter 19

ABOVE AND BEYOND

**Don't assume that I came to destroy the Law or the Prophets.
I did not come to destroy but to fulfill.**

MATTHEW 5:17

JESUS WAS NO ordinary teacher.

He didn't belong to the order of the scribes or Pharisees, the religious elite of the day. He wasn't an official "doctor of the law." And yet he talked about the law in a more penetrating fashion than anyone had ever done before, not hesitating to be critical of the so-called experts.

Perhaps more than his words, though, many were baffled by his conduct. He didn't observe the Sabbath in keeping with their oral traditions. He didn't enforce their time-honored rules about fasting. Most disconcerting of all, he associated with sinners— people who rendered him ceremonially unclean.

Some misconstrued this to mean that he was indicating there were no rules at all. This confusion remains to this day, maintained by those who suggest that Jesus abolished the law and introduced an era of grace. We can hear it when someone argues, "I don't have to do that. I'm under grace, not the law."

Yet Jesus could stand before his disciples and tell them, "Don't assume that I came to destroy the Law or the Prophets. I did not come to destroy but to fulfill." From the sound of it, he was endorsing the backbreaking law-abiding of the religious hard-liners, advocating a lifestyle of sterile legalism.

No, Jesus was no ordinary teacher.

But is there any way to understand what he meant by this confusing statement? What relationship to the Old Testament law does the kingdom person have?

JESUS FULFILLED THE LAW

Jesus made his relationship to his Father's law quite explicit: he came to fulfill it and not abolish it.

He fulfilled "the Law" by living in complete obedience to its original design and purpose. And he fulfilled "the Prophets" by completing all the promises that had been made about him in their writings.

He was "born under the law" (Gal. 4:4), fulfilled the law in his life and teaching, bore the "curse of the law" by his death on the cross (Gal. 3:13), and continues to fulfill "the law's requirement" through believers today as he enables us to walk by the Spirit (Rom. 8:3–4).

Jesus fulfilled and upheld the law. Period.

In truth, the ones most guilty of *destroying* the law were the teachers of the law themselves! They were always trying to find a loophole that would enable them to obey the *letter* of the law while at the same time ignoring its spirit and true intent. Jesus compared them to whitewashed tombs, people who kept up a clean appearance on the outside but who were dead on the inside (Matt. 23:27–28). Warren Wiersbe wrote, "The Pharisees thought they were *cons*erving God's Word, when in reality they were *pre*serving God's Word, embalming it so that it no longer had any life."[1]

Most especially, they were destroying the law through their rejection of God's Messiah—the One to whom the Law and the Prophets had pointed—and were preventing others from experiencing an entrance into God's kingdom. As Jesus said, "Woe to you, scribes and Pharisees, hypocrites! You lock up the kingdom of heaven from people. For you don't go in, and you don't allow those entering to go in" (Matt. 23:13).

Jesus understood that the purpose of God's law was to promote holy living among God's people. Thus, he desired that kingdom citizens love it, learn it, and live it (Matt. 5:19). He made this possible in several ways:

1. *He simplified it,* rescuing it from all the traditions of man, which had been added on over the years and were being used as a way to control and manipulate.

2. *He intensified it,* moving it from mere outward conformity to inner desire, giving kingdom citizens a righteousness that exceeded that of even the Pharisees.

3. *He internalized it,* writing it on our hearts and giving us the Holy Spirit, who enables us to obey it joyfully.

It's true that there are many parts of the ceremonial law which were fulfilled in Christ and are therefore no longer binding on God's people. These were "a shadow of what was to come; the substance is the Messiah" (Col. 2:17). But if we want to be "great in the kingdom of heaven" (Matt. 5:19), we must have a desire to learn, love, and obey the law of God.

In fact, we must go above and beyond.

SURPASSING RIGHTEOUSNESS

I touched on this in chapter 15, but I want to reinforce it here because it is absolutely liberating. In Matthew 5:21–48, Jesus took six important Old Testament laws and applied them in terms of daily kingdom living, making clear that the Father was not concerned about technicalities but about transformed hearts. He was focusing on prevention rather than punishment.

These six teachings—on topics like anger, lust, and loving our enemies—are more than just ethical lessons. If Jesus' goal was to give us a comprehensive code of conduct, he wouldn't have stopped with these half-dozen entries. He would have covered far more. His desire, however, was to use these six examples to show that *all* of our behavior and attitudes have one motivating factor. And it's found in the wrap-up of Matthew 5—"so that you may be sons of your Father in heaven" (v. 45).

Our obedience gives evidence of our relationship.

In some ways, yes, these are impossible ideals. But for the kingdom person, our desire is not to make a certain grade or to scratch marks off a checklist. We are being enabled to obey by a God who is "perfect" (v. 48). And by living to please him, our lives are not bound by laws but freed by love.

We don't obey because we *have* to. We obey because we *want* to.

So, for example:

We want to love and respect others (vv. 21–26). Most of us feel comfortable with the command not to murder. But Jesus shattered our self-righteousness by asserting that being angry with another person is just as bad.

We shouldn't see this as judgment, however, on every passing, angry thought. The present-tense verb he used in this passage suggests a "continuous action of anger," a settled grudge we inwardly nurture and tenaciously cling to—the sort of seething anger that's liable to erupt in harsh name-calling. Such angry insults were a serious issue in Jesus' day, much more shameful than two kids squaring off on the playground. Theirs was an honor-and-shame society. If a person were to lose his good reputation, it was about the same as dying. So to call someone a "fool" in public was nearly the same as dispatching him to the fires of hell.

Jesus insisted that kingdom people must deal with their anger quickly and privately, not through public potshots but through private restoration. How can we come to the place of worship, for example—the place where we seek and celebrate our reconciliation with God—while we are stubbornly harboring a grudge with our brother? Unsettled anger imprisons us in bitterness, blocks the joy of our worship, and disrupts our kingdom fellowship.

We want to keep ourselves sexually pure (vv. 27–30). Sex is one of God's great gifts to mankind, created not only for procreation but also for enjoyment. His purpose in regulating sex is not to rob us of its pleasure but to protect its blessings in our lives. This is why Jesus urged his followers to maintain their sexual purity at the very point where it begins its initial descent into debauchery—the lustful look.

Contrary to the normal religious teaching of his day, Jesus didn't condemn his disciples for being attracted to women, which is simply part of our human design. He didn't say not to *look*. He said not to *leer*. It's not the casual glance that entraps a man but the focused stare, the deliberate decision to feed the sensual appetite. This lustful look has two elements of danger and disobedience:

- It dehumanizes the woman, created in God's image, making her an object of desire rather than a person of worth.
- It leads man into sin. What begins in the heart and mind is often acted upon through our behavior.

Few things give us greater freedom and a stronger kingdom testimony in our day than sexual purity. This is why Jesus directed his followers to deal with this matter decisively and immediately. When he talked about cutting off the hand and gouging out the eye, he wasn't teaching self-mutilation (of course) but emphasizing the fact that sexual sin cannot be gradually tapered off. It must be cut off! Our Father's reputation is at stake.

We want to keep our marriage vows (vv. 31–32). Divorce in biblical times was often an independent action on the man's part to rid himself of an unwanted wife. The rabbis of Jesus' day liked to debate the legal scenarios for divorce (Matt. 19:1–9), and some used Moses' instructions about the delivery of the "certificate of divorce" (Deut. 24:1–4) as convenient permission for ending an undesirable marriage.

Jesus undercut this self-righteous rationale by reminding them that Moses made this "certificate" exception as a compromise based on the "hardness of your hearts" (19:8), which hardly made it an honorable precedent to build one's case around. Jesus focused instead on God's original plan: one man and one woman, bound together for a lifetime (19:4–7).

The divorce statistics in our country continue to mount, and tragically there is little difference when we compare the numbers in the church with those of society at-large. God hates divorce because it creates untold suffering for his children—and for *their* children—who were created for blessing and as a witness to the world. But we must always remember that God's heart breaks for those who are divorced, who have placed their marriages in peril by succumbing to sinful situations or whose lives have been upended by an unfaithful or irresponsible spouse. The kingdom-focused church should continually affirm the permanence of marriage while at the same time offering full mercy and forgiveness to those who have suffered from failed relationships.

We want to be people of integrity (vv. 33–37). The rabbis of Jesus' day loved to have hair-splitting discussions about the relative value of different oaths or vows. Such matters commanded many pages in the Mishnah, a collection of rabbinic teachings. The Pharisees, who were unmatched in their ability to weave grandiose reasons for sidestepping the truth, found this issue of oath-making a fertile playground for their evasive schemes and strategies. They would scrupulously avoid swearing by the name of God, but they would substitute something like heaven, the throne of God, the earth, Jerusalem—or even the head on their own shoulders—all to get their verbal point across and still remain six inches inside the law (Matt. 5:34–36).

Jesus cut to the chase. The use of oaths could never compensate for a lack of integrity. The need for an oath was an admission of failure in some area of truthfulness. Kingdom citizens, Jesus said, don't need to swear by anything! Their *yes* means *yes,* and their *no* means *no.* They speak the truth because their Father is the *author* of truth.

So if you tell someone you're going to be somewhere or accomplish a certain task, can they depend on you? Does your employer know that you'll give a good day's work whether anyone is observing you or not? Truthfulness should characterize every area of the kingdom person's life.

We want a spirit of humility (vv. 38–42). The Mosaic Law stipulated an "eye for an eye" and a "tooth for a tooth" to keep people from forcing an offender to pay a much higher price than his offense merited. Jesus moved beyond this law by calling his people to a spirit of humility, instructing the offended party not to resort to retaliation.

These admonitions to turn the other cheek and to walk the second mile do not mean that we should never resist evil, nor do they mean that we should submit to injustice in our society. But they do require us to check our hearts, to see if our first response to evil or aggression is to return it in kind.

The actions of kingdom citizens are designed to stop the escalation of violence. We should be willing to suffer loss rather than cause another to suffer. We should not only know but actively live out the promise that vengeance belongs to a holy God who is perfect in his retribution (Rom. 12:19). And we should be willing to forego legitimate rights if it's helpful in the spread of the gospel (1 Cor. 9:12).

Kingdom people are peacemakers, not backbiters.

We want to be perfect in love (vv. 38–42). You won't find any admonition in Old Testament law that encourages a person to hate his enemy. But the Old Testament does make a clear distinction between one's attitude toward both his fellow Israelite and the non-Israelite. It appears that this distinction may have been twisted by some to condone a hatred of Gentiles. But Jesus demanded a love that does not discriminate. This doesn't mean we have to like the things some people do—*or even like the people themselves,* as far as having feelings of affection toward them. But love demands that we be concerned for the welfare of our enemies and pray for them.

Who knows? You may even start to *like* them too! God's done it before!

Again, these six statements are not do-or-die lists. These are simply the Spirit-led desires that well up inside the hearts of kingdom people, making them want to please their Father and help others recognize our Father-son, Father-daughter relationship.

When we love our enemy, for example, we are behaving like our Father. "For if, while we were enemies, we were reconciled to God through the death of His Son, then how much more, having been reconciled, will we be saved by His life!" (Rom. 5:10). If we love only those who love us back, how do people see the kingdom difference in us?

Does God expect us to do this perfectly? No.

In the Hebrew way of thinking, something was considered "perfect" if it fulfilled the task for which it was created. That's why the Bible can truthfully refer to men like Noah (Gen. 6:9) and Job (Job 1:8) as being "perfect"—not because they'd achieved moral or religious perfection but because they were wholeheartedly committed to God. They were serving their purpose.

And so are we—the kingdom purposes of embracing God's mission, embodying God's name, and obeying God's Word—above and beyond the call of duty.

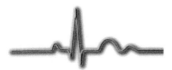

Kids from all walks of life are having sex at younger and younger ages. Nearly 1 in 10 reports losing his or her virginity before the age of 13, a 15 percent increase since 1997, according to the Centers for Disease Control and Prevention. And despite a solid 20 percent decrease in the teen birthrate between 1991 and 1999, 20 percent of sexually active girls 15 to 19 get pregnant each year, according to the Henry J. Kaiser Family Foundation. (Source: U.S.News and World Report, 27 May 2002)

- Do you think the 10 Commandments are relevant today? Why/why not?
- What evidence do you see in daily life that many people are angry?
- Is sexual purity an outdated value in today's world?
- Who are your enemies? Did you ever think about loving them?

Chapter 20

WHERE'S MY REWARD?

Be careful not to practice your righteousness in front of people, to be seen by them. Otherwise, you will have no reward from your Father in heaven.

MATTHEW 6:1

IT WAS MY FINAL YEAR in Little League baseball. I was the catcher during that season and had gotten to be pretty reliable behind the plate.

It was a good thing, too, because it certainly wasn't my *bat* that was keeping me in the starting lineup. Not only could I not make regular contact, but I had never been able to hit for power. All the accolades went to those players who could hit the home runs. And it appeared that I would finish my career without a single round-tripper.

Only a few of my childhood memories are so clearly etched in my mind that when I rerun them, I experience them again in full color and surround sound.

But the night I hit my home run is like that.

I can still see the ball barely clearing the center-field fence. I remember trotting around the bases as if on a victory lap. What is most vivid to me is the memory of my dad's face when I rounded third base. He wasn't hard to spot because he was running down the third base line with me. The smile etched on his face illuminated the park as he shouted, "That's my boy!"

Numerous studies have proven the importance of parental approval in the healthy development of a child. As a pastor, however, I've never needed research books to convince me how accurate this assessment is. On numerous occasions I have seen teens and adults acting out in rather strange ways because they had never sensed the approval of their parents. I've sat in the counseling room and heard them tearfully confess how their achievements were never enough to impress their moms or dads.

We do seek and need approval in order to be healthy people, but the question is this: Whose approval do you most desire? The approval of men or the approval of your heavenly Father? Even if you've been forced to endure the tragic, unfortunate experience of being denied a father's approval, can the Lord give you the satisfaction and fulfillment of being rewarded by your one true Dad?

Can his smile ever be enough?

THREE ROADS TO SURE REWARD

The word *beware* always warns us of danger ahead, like a bridge being out of order or a road being under water. To refuse to heed such a sign is both foolish and dangerous. But as the middle chapter of the Sermon on the Mount—Matthew 6—begins, the first words out of Jesus' mouth are these: "Be careful."

Beware!

As kingdom people intent on obeying the Word of God, we know we cannot tread lightly upon the following matters if we wish to please our Father. As we hear Jesus begin to teach his disciples a few things about the way they should approach their religious activity, we too must listen reverently—and be prepared to obey completely—if we're to receive our Father's reward.

The three issues Jesus discussed in the first part of Matthew 6—fasting, prayer, and giving—were at the heart of the Jewish religion. And they're still important aspects of kingdom living today:

- Fasting prepares us for powerful prayer.
- Prayer moves us to generosity.
- Generous giving provides visible evidence of our relationship to God.[1]

And much to the dismay of the Pharisees—and for the benefit of all the rest of us who struggle with this from time to time—Jesus was not about to gloss over any one of these matters without confronting us on the issue of motive.

Fasting. When we think of fasting, we most often think of skipping a meal or two for prayer. But in truth, skipping a meal is only a *symbol* of fasting. The underlying issue is far greater, deeper, and more profound than a single missed meal.

When I was pastor at First Baptist Church in Norfolk, Virginia, we frequently called our congregation to prayer and fasting. On several occasions we invited our members to gather at the church during their lunch hour for prayer. I'll never forget the testimony of one of our senior adults, who shared something he had learned after several days of fasting. He related how he had left the house at lunchtime on his way to church, beginning to pray in his camper. And while he was praying, he became acutely aware of his physical hunger. He realized, of course, that these hunger pains were more mental than physical since he was in no real danger of experiencing *serious hunger.* He knew he had fully stocked pantries waiting at home, once his fast was over. But in this king-dom moment, he realized he didn't have the same hunger for God that he did for food. His "hunger for righteousness" didn't gnaw at him with the same regularity and intensity as his hunger for breakfast, lunch, and dinner.

This man had discovered the true meaning of fasting. Fasting is nothing more than a *passionate hunger to know God in greater intimacy.* It is the denial of anything—of everything—that inter-feres with direct fellowship between the Father and us.

Often, though, because we can be so slow to act and so quick to forget, we need the physical symbol of fasting—such as the skipping of a meal—in order to remind us of this kingdom truth. But missing lunch is not really the point!

The Pharisees made an external display of their fasting. They put on a gloomy face and neglected their appearance in order to impress men with the level of their religious devotion (6:16–18). And since that's all they really wanted, God seemed willing to let them have it.

But they'd better enjoy it because whatever thrills they received from attracting other people's attention was all the reward they were going to get.

And it works the same with us. Do we hunger for God, or do we hunger for others to recognize us? Do we yearn to go deeper into his presence with consistent regularity? Are we willing to give up anything that obstructs our fellowship with him?

Then we're getting to the heart of fasting.

Prayer. The hunger for God that grows inside of us during fast-ing paves the way for prayer—meaningful prayer, passionate prayer, personal prayer. When we understand that the sovereign

God of the universe invites us to enter his presence in prayer and to address him as Father, it transforms our praying. It's no longer a religious duty. It's now a personal privilege, sweet communication between Father and child.

When my youngest daughter, Katie, left for college, she developed the habit of calling home on a regular basis. I've jokingly stated that her phone bill exceeded her tuition! I'd be driving down the road, and my cell phone would ring. She'd greet me with her standard opening line: "Whatcha doing?" At first I'd think she might be sick or needing money. But soon I'd realize she just wanted to talk to her dad. So do you know what I did? I bought her a cell phone with hundreds of monthly minutes! I wanted her to know she could call me any time she wanted!

The sovereign God of the universe has given you the same thing—only better!—a direct line of communication to him with unlimited minutes and no chance of ever being disconnected. You don't have to wander around asking, "Can you hear me now?" He can hear you just fine. And he wants to hear from you a lot!

Hypocrites never understand this—now or in Jesus' day. He said they prayed "to be seen by people" (Matt. 6:5). Don't you find it curious that the text doesn't say they prayed to be *heard* by people? No, the content of their prayer was of little concern to them. It was all about appearances for the Pharisees.

But as children of God, we can live without the worry and pretense of craving the applause of other people. All we want is the opportunity to meet with our Father in the inner room of our hearts, to look for time throughout the day to talk to our heavenly Dad.

Giving. As a result of enjoying intimate communication with the Father, we're quickly able to spot opportunities to pour out our resources into kingdom causes—and to sense his freedom and direction in doing so. Cheerful, generous giving is clear evidence of our desire to surrender our whole lives in selfless service to our Father.

Do you recall the result of Isaiah's first memorable encounter with his heavenly Father? The Lord cried out to him in Three-in-One splendor, "Who should I send? Who will go for Us?" And Isaiah answered, "Here I am. Send me" (Isa. 6:8).

When you spend time in your Father's presence, you'll begin to see the world from his perspective. Your spirit will be transformed to share his concern for the nations. Your lifestyle, calendar, and checkbook will clearly reflect your understanding of the Father's heart and your desire to please him with everything you own.

The Pharisees gave their tokens of charitable goodwill, to be sure, but like just about everything else, they did it to garner the praise of men. Sometimes one of them would position himself in a conspicuous, visible place. He might even go so far as to blow a small silver trumpet, signaling the lame and the blind to gather around him, hands spread wide to beg for his aid. With great fanfare, the Pharisee would scatter his gifts among them, caring little or nothing about either their need or their future.[2]

Jesus' response concerning these haughty hypocrites was crisp and clear: "They've got their reward!" (Matt. 6:2).

Let's *beware,* though! It would be easy to leave this section thinking ill of the Pharisees without confronting these issues on a more personal level. Does our love for the Father cause us to remove any impediment to fellowship with him? What if it meant turning off the television at night or getting up an hour earlier? Does our time in prayer with him cause us to respond generously to others with our time and money? Are we investing wisely in the kingdom of God?

We always need to keep a tight check on our motives because we don't want our reward held up by our hypocrisy.

DAD'S SUFFICIENT REWARD

As a pastor, I've heard just about all the reasons people can give for why they don't give or go or serve. Often their hesitance is related to some real or imagined slight they've received. Perhaps they had volunteered to serve, and no one called them back. Or they served in some capacity at one time, but no one noticed or complimented them. People come up with a wide assortment of excuses, but they all boil down to this: a lack of motive and passion.

Kingdom people, however, serve and give for one primary reason: the love we have for our Father compels us to do so.

Do you remember how John the apostle introduced the coming of Jesus? He said Jesus was the "true light" who came into the world to give "light to everyone." But when Jesus arrived on the earth, "the world did not know Him. He came to His own, and His own people did not receive Him" (John 1:9–11). How could Jesus face this kind of rejection? How could he stand to be mocked and scorned by the very people he'd given his life to redeem? Because he knew he had his Father's approval.

And that was enough.

I know that some readers don't pay much attention to the footnotes in a book, but twice in this chapter, I've quoted from a commentary on the Gospel of Matthew written by G. Campbell Morgan. This great Congregationalist pastor of the early twentieth century pastored numerous churches, including the prestigious Westminster Chapel of London. He traveled extensively preaching to large crowds, and his literary output was immense. Yet his beginning in the ministry was fraught with rejection.

The day his name appeared on the rejection list of the Methodist church, which essentially excluded him from the pulpit, his diary entry read, "Very dark everything seems. Still, He knoweth best." That same day, he sent a telegram to his father, containing one word: "Rejected." But his father sent back a wise reply: "Rejected on Earth. Accepted in heaven. Dad."[3]

What else really matters?

The Eternal Question

Will it be the kingdoms of the world and the glory of men, or the kingdom of God and the reward of our Father?

This is the ultimate question for kingdom people.

You may recognize this as the dilemma Jesus faced in his third temptation or testing. But this question was not reserved for him alone. It's the same question we all face every day.

It's the question we preachers must ask ourselves if we're serious about keeping our motives pure and kingdom focused. "Do I prepare and preach for the glory of men, or for my Father's reward? Is his reward enough to motivate me to do my best? What if no one in my church or denomination ever recognizes my service? Will I still be fulfilled?"

I remember when I faced this issue head-on. It was the first time I had ever been asked to preach for a large gathering where many of my peers would be in the audience, and I found myself agonizing about the message and poring over the commentaries. This kingdom question struck me, though—even then. I had to ask myself why I was giving so much more attention to this message than any of the others I had preached to my own little congregation. Was it for any reason other than impressing my peers?

Motive does matter. For all of us.

- Sunday school teachers, instrumentalists, soloists—all who stand in the spotlight—must constantly ask themselves whether they serve for the pleasure of their Father or the compliments of their friends.

- Why should a man want to be a deacon or an elder in his church? Is it just another accomplishment for his spiritual resumé, or is it selfless service for his Dad's honor?

- Anyone who serves or ministers in the church must stop to consider: "Does it bother me when no one notices my work or when someone else receives the credit?"

But we can't leave this matter to church activities alone. Why do you go to work each day? What drives you out of the bed? What motivates you to climb the corporate ladder?

Some of you may be thinking, *Well, I like to eat!* Cute, but that's not good enough! The Father has already promised us daily bread from his own hand.

Do money or awards motivate you? Do you find it satisfying when your walls are lined with certificates and plaques? All of these motivations are doomed to leave us unsatisfied, because there will always be someone who's accumulated more.

Please don't miss my point! I'm not suggesting that you shouldn't ever want to achieve or seek advancement. You should always want to do your best. But your motivation for advancement should be the *advancement of the kingdom and your Father's reward.*

Do you go to your place of business thinking that God can use your profession as a platform for kingdom activity? Are you looking for opportunities to join God at work wherever you are? Do you rejoice over your raise not only because it will help meet the needs of your family but also because God has provided you greater resources to invest in kingdom advancement? Do you seek your Father's approval over anything else on earth?

There's good news when you do. "Your Father who sees in secret will reward you" (Matt. 6:4).

And for the kingdom person, that's good enough.

- How does what you value determine your reward?
- When have you witnessed righteous acts being their own reward?
- Has this ever happened to you?

SECTION 5

His Kingdom Lives

Chapter 21

KINGDOM PRAYER

Therefore, you should pray like this.

MATTHEW 6:9

A FEW YEARS AGO I began a prayer quest that led me once again to the familiar passage known as the Lord's Prayer. Though I had read and recited it countless times, I had never been so struck by the importance of what it had to say. I found myself attracted both by its simplicity and by its radical nature.

As I prayed it, I had to ask myself some serious, personal questions:

- Was I satisfied with daily bread, with just enough for today?
- Did I hallow my Father's name? Was I aware that I represented his name everywhere I went?
- Did I really want God to forgive me in the same meager portion that I was willing to forgive others?
- Did I place his kingdom before my own needs?

Perhaps, in fact, this is where my desire to know more about the kingdom of God first began in earnest because throughout this prayer Jesus drew his disciples' attention to the kingdom—his *hunger* for the kingdom, his daily *awareness* of the kingdom, his *confidence* in the kingdom.

Read the prayer of Jesus carefully enough, and you begin to see that the kingdom of God breathes through every oft-quoted line and phrase.

Most commentators, in fact, agree that the Lord's Prayer is at the heart of the Sermon on the Mount and therefore at the heart of our Lord's teaching on the kingdom of God. *If for no other reason than this,* we should hunger afresh to understand its impact.

I can only say that studying the Lord's Prayer has changed my life. I came to it in the hopes that God would use it to improve my experience in prayer, and instead he has used it not only to alter my prayer life but to transform my view of the world. Through this powerful prayer, the Father has sensitized me to his kingdom activity and has given me the courage to participate with him as he advances his kingdom through me.

I can't wait to see and hear what this prayer does in your life, as well.[1]

"OUR FATHER IN HEAVEN"

We're probably so familiar with this opening line that the full impact of its radical nature doesn't startle us the way it did Jesus' first-century disciples. The intimacy of address Jesus used in approaching God as "Father" is our first signal to the radical nature of this prayer. No one in Jesus' day would've ever *dared* address the Creator and King as "our Father." This level of personal intimacy was unheard of.

But it wasn't an accident on Jesus' part. Nor was it descriptive only of the relationship he had with the Father as the result of being his Son. For Jesus would later tell his disciples,

"Anything *you* ask the Father in my name, He will give *you*" (John 16:23).

All of his children were invited into this relationship.

I received Christ as my personal Savior when I was nine years of age. In that moment, as I prayed to accept Christ into my heart, my sins were forgiven, I was transferred from the kingdom of darkness into the kingdom of life, and my home in heaven was assured.

But I can see in my mind's eye one other significant event that occurred. Jesus took me by the hand and led me into the presence of sovereign God. He whispered to me, "Look, Ken, some call him Yahweh, the God of covenant faithfulness. But I just call him Dad. And now that you're in relationship with me, you too can climb up into his lap and address him as Dad."

I hope you know that I would in no way trivialize God's transcendence. I'm not meaning to make him any less than he should be in our eyes. I'm meaning to make him *more!* This is not an issue of irreverence. It is an issue of intimacy.

Paul said that when we received the gift of the Holy Spirit, he gave us the right to cry out, "Abba, Father" (Rom. 8:15), a word that actually carries the meaning of our word *Daddy.* This is a testimony to God's love and grace, not an offensive devaluation of his holiness. It took a great God to stoop down to us, to desire to be our Father.

His Hallowed Name

Jesus, for certain, considered his Father's name holy. We know this from the next line of the Lord's Prayer. When we pray "hallowed be thy name," we are not giving God permission for his name to be holy. *His name is holy already*—so holy, in fact, that when Jews came to the name YHWH (Jehovah) in the Scripture text, they would not speak it aloud for fear of mispronouncing it. In the Book of Revelation, we are told that the living creatures around the Father's throne never cease in crying, "Holy, holy, holy, Lord God, the Almighty, who was, who is, and who is coming" (4:8).

So we're not asking for God's name to be made holy in its very nature. It already is! We're asking for his name to be made holy in our lives.

To understand the significance of this kingdom commitment, think back to God's purpose in the redemption of Israel. "God came to one nation on earth in order to redeem a people for Himself, to make a name for Himself" (2 Sam. 7:23). He was seeking a people who would exhibit his holiness among the nations in order that the world would be drawn to him. But as we know from Israel's history, "when they came to the nations where they went, they profaned [His] holy name" (Ezek. 36:20). The nations concluded, then—by looking at Israel's conduct and behavior—that God's name was *not* hallowed.

Yet once again God declared to manifest his holiness to the world by proving himself holy among his people. In Jesus' farewell prayer before going to the cross, he told the Father, "I have revealed Your name to the men You gave Me from the world" (John 17:6). In other words, Jesus succeeded where Israel had failed. Every action, word, and deed of his life had been built around a singular focus—to reveal his Father's name. "I made Your name known to them and will make it known, so that the love with which You have loved Me may be in them, and that I may be in them" (17:26).

Did you notice the evangelistic intent in Jesus' words? Why did he want the world to know how much his Father loved him? So they could experience this same love for themselves.

I had read this verse numerous times before it dawned on me that when Jesus said he *would* make the Father's name known, he was referring to the one, big event that remained in his future: the cross. Jesus' only concern was that when the events of the scourging and crucifixion unfolded, he would respond in such a way that he would manifest his Father's holy name. So when the pagan centurion declared at the foot of the cross, "This man really was God's Son" (Matt. 27:54), he was simply recognizing the family resemblance.

Not long ago, after I had delivered a sermon, a gentleman approached me who had known my dad and had heard him preach many times. He remarked how much my voice sounded like my dad's, how our characteristics were so much alike. He said to me, "While you were preaching, I closed my eyes and listened, and it was like I could hear your father preaching again."

I have never had a nicer, more meaningful compliment paid to me. It should be like that when others see us. They should see and hear and experience our Father.

If we are committed to being kingdom people, we too must constantly be asking the Father to hallow his name in our lives. We must recognize that everywhere we go and everything we do has an impact on our Father's name and the credibility of our witness. So we must pray for him to protect our mouths and direct our behavior so that his name will be hallowed and not profaned in our lives.

Thy Kingdom Come

Perhaps the most direct passage in the Lord's Prayer concerning our kingdom purpose is this one: "Thy kingdom come." And it needs to be viewed through the same lens as the "hallowed be thy name" commitment. We are not assuming that the kingdom's arrival is somehow in question. The final consummation of the kingdom is an established, biblical fact.

Our prayer that God's kingdom will "come" is an appeal for its reality to be evident in our daily lives.

When I pray this line from the Lord's Prayer, I am establishing that my first concern each day is *God's* kingdom and not mine. Further, I am asking the Father to show me what he is doing and allow me to participate with him as he advances his kingdom on earth.

To me, this is the most exciting and challenging aspect of the prayer.

Let me illustrate this in the life of Jesus. Remember the time when he had healed a man on the Sabbath, and the Jewish leaders were persecuting him for it? Jesus' response to them may have seemed a bit of an enigma. He said, "My Father is still working, and I also am working" (John 5:17). Let me offer the Hemphill paraphrase: "You guys are upset about me healing this guy on the Sabbath? Then take it up with my Father! I didn't initiate this event. My Father was already healing the guy, and I simply said, 'Dad, if you're going to heal him, can I share in the celebration?'"

If you think I'm reading a bit much into the context, keep reading from verses 19–20: "I assure you: The Son is not able to do anything on His own, but only what He sees the Father doing. For whatever the Father does, these things the Son also does in the same way. For the Father loves the Son and shows Him everything He is doing."

Here we find not only the key to understanding Jesus' ministry but also the key for understanding what it means for us to pray "thy kingdom come." Jesus did not set his own agenda. He simply looked for his Father's activity and joined him where he was working. Thus he was not flustered, for example, when the woman with the issue of blood (Mark 5:25–36) grabbed his cloak while he was actually on his way elsewhere, to restore the daughter of Jairus from death. He knew that this "interruption" was his Father's activity.

Once when I was reading this verse—John 5:20—I was prompted to ask the Father why he didn't show me everything he was doing around me. His response was profound but convicting: I had never really asked him to do so.

Have you?

I can promise you, he will show you. And as a result, if you will remain observant and obedient, you will never have another boring day. You'll begin to see kingdom activity everywhere. It's sort of like the *Where's Waldo?* books or those *Magic Eye* puzzles they used to put in the Sunday comics. You can look at them and stare sideways at them and see nothing for a long time. But once you know what you're looking for, you can't miss it. That's sort of the way life in the Spirit works.

My dad was a Baptist minister, and therefore I grew up in the church. I actually loved to attend. And I wanted to see God at work. I invited my friends to church, witnessed to them, gave my tithe, and sang in the youth choir. But I had divided life into two separate piles—the sacred and the secular. Somehow I had never fully comprehended the fact that God was at work all around me all the time, advancing his kingdom, wanting me to join him anywhere I happened to be.

This point came vividly home to me one day as I stepped out of my office door at Southwestern Baptist Seminary, heading toward the chapel to preach. I had assumed that delivering this message would be my kingdom activity of the morning. Still, I remember breathing a request that the Father would show me where he was at work.

As I walked down the hall, I passed a young man who looked like a deer in headlights. Noticing but not stopping, I grunted a "how's it going?" in his general direction, not really meaning it. Then the Holy Spirit stopped me in my tracks. I turned and walked back to the student, and I asked him again: "How's it going? I really want to know." His eyes filled with tears. Here was a young man struggling with direction in his life. He was trying to follow God's will by being enrolled in seminary, but his wife had required several back surgeries, and their funds were scarce. He was nearly at the end of his rope. I stopped and prayed with him, and I invited both him and his wife to come by my office that afternoon to talk things over. It was a kingdom moment.

I had no idea about his need or pain when I passed him that morning. But my Father did. And all God needed was a movable possession willing to say, "Thy kingdom come, thy will be done."

Really, you cannot pray, "Thy kingdom come," until you're prepared to pray, "Thy will be done." When we ask God to accomplish his will "on earth as it is in heaven," we are pledging our unconditional obedience. *And our willingness to obey is what enables us to see the Father's kingdom activity.* When we are disobedient, we forfeit the incredible privilege of seeing what the Father is doing to advance his kingdom.

I can promise you from personal experience, you don't want to miss out on kingdom activity. You can watch as it invades your personal life throughout the day, every day.

And it is thrilling!

Have you ever asked God to show you everything he is doing? Try it today! Ask him to give you the ability to showcase his name and obey him.

OPENING PRAYER

What does it mean to pray in Jesus' name? It first means that we've established a personal relationship with God through his Son. But further, it means that we address the Father with the *same commitment and mission* as his Son. It means that his Son's passion has become our priority.

- It is the confident prayer of a child who knows his Father is in the heavens, far beyond all that we will ever comprehend, yet nonetheless so near that he knows what we need before we ask him.
- This is the prayer of the child who knows his Father's name is holy and whose passion is to manifest the Father's holiness in his own life.
- It's the prayer of the child who knows that his Father's kingdom is paramount and whose first desire is to advance that kingdom.

- It's the prayer of the child who knows his Father is trustworthy, and therefore he submits his will to that of the Father.
- It's the prayer of the child whose only desire is to enjoy his Father's reward.

Two-thirds of the Lord's Prayer addresses the issues of the Father, and only one-third speaks of our personal needs. In thinking about my own prayer life, I realized that I had often reversed that order. I usually spent the largest amount of my prayer time on my own needs and wants.

But kingdom praying is not about informing God. He already knows!

Kingdom praying is not about convincing God to side with us. He already has!

Kingdom praying is about enjoying God's presence and discovering his purpose.

Is that what you're already doing—or are ready with all of your heart to start doing today?

 *Contradictions and confusion permeate the spiritual condition of the nation. Studies conducted during 2003 indicate, for instance, that while 84 percent of adults say their religious faith is very important in their own life, 66 percent also say that religion is losing influence in the nation. While people are clearly spending less time involved in religious practices such as Bible reading,*

*prayer, and participating in church activities, 70 percent claim
that their own religious faith is consistently growing deeper.*

*Further, at the same time that 84 percent of adults claim to
be Christian, three out of four say they are either absolutely or
somewhat committed to Christianity, and three-fifths say they
believe the Bible is totally accurate in all that it teaches, the
moral foundations of the nation are crumbling. This year
brought about increases in the proportions of people who
contend that cohabitation (60%), adultery (42%), sexual
relations between homosexuals (30%), abortion (45%),
pornography (38%), the use of profanity (36%) and gambling
(61%) are "morally acceptable" behaviors.* (Source: "Spiritual
Progress Hard to Find in 2003," December 22, 2003, Barna
Research Online, http://www.barna.org/cgi-bin/ PagePress
Release.asp?PressReleaseID=155&Reference=E&Key=prayer)

- If you wanted someone to pray for you, whom would you call? Why?
- How meaningful is your prayer life?
- How would "kingdom praying" change your prayer life?

Chapter 22

THREE POINTS AND A PURPOSE

**For Yours is the kingdom and
the power and the glory forever, Amen.**

MATTHEW 6:13

I'VE BEEN ENCOURAGED by the many people who have been drawn to Rick Warren's book *The Purpose Driven Life.* The fact that a lot of us are giving serious thought as to why we're here on Earth is a hopeful sign because this issue is one we all must settle if we're to enjoy a meaningful life, if we're to become kingdom people.

Whether we recognize it or not, we all live by some sort of purpose statement. It may not be written down or carefully formulated, but we function with one nonetheless.

Some people, of course, still work under the false assumption that life's purpose is wrapped up in accomplishment, wealth, and recognition—in cool toys and job titles. Most of us know better than to admit this outright, but how many of us spend the bulk of our time chasing these very things . . . or at least wishing we had them?

For many others, though, life is just about survival. They live from vacation to vacation, merely wanting to make it to another payday and hoping they have enough left over to retire on. That's about it.

Right after I graduated from Cambridge, I taught for a year at Wingate College in North Carolina. I had one particularly bright student who refused to apply himself, and though I tried my best to motivate him, I couldn't seem to break through his shell. So one day after class, I just came right out and asked him why he was willing to waste his talents and opportunities like this. He said something like, "Aw, life's a bummer. You attend a *school* you don't like to get a *job* you won't like. You work your whole life to earn enough to retire, and when you finally do, you die."

No wonder he wasn't motivated.

But that's the way a lot of people see their lives—pouring everything into a pointless exercise that eventually leaks out and leaves them with nothing. And so if that's all there is, I agree with them. If life is nothing more than a war for survival—and if death is the only prize you get for winning—why even join the battle? Who can argue with the logic?

Kingdom people can.

We, too, believe this earth is a temporary kingdom that's destined to pass away. We, too, don't know why anyone would want to invest all their energies and efforts into building something that's so flimsy and fleeting.

But we believe there's a better way.

We believe in a kingdom, and a power, and a glory that goes on forever.

And we're not settling for anything less.

THINE IS THE KINGDOM

Because I believe the Lord's Prayer is so central to our understanding of the kingdom of God and our ability to live it out, I want to spend this whole chapter looking at its final line, which is rich with meaning.

You may have a translation that doesn't include this benediction, or which indicates that it's not found in some of the earliest manuscripts. Because of research findings and because of the absence of this wording in Luke's version of the prayer, some commentators have concluded that this closing line—"For Yours is the kingdom and the power and the glory forever"—was not original. Whether it was or not, I don't know. But it certainly is appropriate to the prayer, and it is definitely consistent with Jesus' teaching.

If nothing else, I think it gives us a wonderful purpose statement for life. It's one of the best answers I know to the question, Why are we here? *We are here to advance God's kingdom through his empowering and for his glory.*

The first phrase, "Thine is the kingdom," is an affirmation we should make daily.

- Every time we start to believe that life revolves around us, we must remind ourselves, "Thine is the kingdom."
- Every time we become worried and anxious, every time we think the solutions to our problems are all up to us, we should declare with confidence, "Thine is the kingdom."
- Every time we're torn about decisions that need to be made and variables that need to be considered, we ought to rest in the fact that "thine is the kingdom."

If God's only purpose in our lives was to redeem us, why wouldn't he just take us up to heaven the moment we were saved? Instead, he leaves us here on Earth with a clear calling and purpose—*to participate in his kingdom activity until he returns.* This is the greatest privilege and desire of the kingdom person, and it fills each day with anticipation and joyful surprise.

For example, you may have a job right now that doesn't offer much in the way of fulfillment. It's not a career choice but a necessary paycheck. And you may be asking God every day to give you a better opportunity. There's nothing wrong with that!

But have you asked God to show you the kingdom opportunities that already exist where you are? Have you ever thought that he might've deliberately placed you in this very job—*you, his movable possession*—to witness to unsaved clients and coworkers? To minister to discouraged believers? To be a Holy Spirit light in the darkness? Instead of complaining while seeking a different job, why not at the same time make the most of every kingdom opportunity in *this* job? You might not believe how many there are!

A member of our church came to me to discuss her job situation. She was a nurse who had accrued enough seniority over the years to be allowed to work day shifts. For some reason, though, she had fallen out of grace with her supervisor. Perhaps it had something to do with her Christian commitment. But whatever the cause, the result was the same. She had been relegated to nights. And she hated it.

By the time she came to me, her change to night duty had begun to affect both her work and her marriage. I understood. We talked. But I did ask her if she'd ever thought that God might have a special reason for her to be on the night shift. I counseled her about her attitude and the possible negative impact it might have on her witness.

When I saw her again several weeks later, I noticed the smile on her face and the bounce in her step. Just from looking at her, I figured she had perhaps been moved back to the day shift. But I was wrong. She told me instead that the slower pace at night—without the constant visits of doctors—had given her an unusual opportunity to minister to her patients. She grew to like it so much, in fact, that when offered the opportunity to return to days, she refused.

And all because "thine is the kingdom"—even in the middle of the night.

THINE IS THE POWER

Perhaps you feel inadequate to accomplish kingdom work! You've always assumed that this is the stuff of missionaries, preachers, and other such superheroes.

I've got news for you: There *are* no superheroes in the kingdom of God. Nobody can do kingdom work in his own strength. Nobody. Kingdom work requires kingdom empowering, and no one can do anything of value without it.

Do you remember what the early disciples were like after the crucifixion? The biblical record is very honest. When Mary came from the tomb with the incredible news that Jesus was alive, his disciples refused to believe it (Mark 16:11). Even after his many resurrection appearances, some still doubted (Matt. 28:17).

So how do we account for the boldness of someone like Peter—the apostle who had denied his Lord three times, barely more than six weeks before—standing and preaching to an entire, impromptu crowd on the day of Pentecost, being used by God to receive three thousand people into the kingdom in a single day?

This wasn't the Peter we knew.

It was the work of the Holy Spirit, whose power had come with the expressed purpose of turning ordinary people like Peter into courageous witnesses for Christ "in Jerusalem, in all Judea and Samaria, and to the ends of the earth" (Acts 1:8).

The Spirit gave these early disciples daily equipping for their kingdom ministry. When they were questioned by the powerful Sanhedrin about the source of their unusual power, the Scripture says that Peter was "filled with the Holy Spirit" as he responded in courage and eloquence (Acts 4:8). This wasn't Peter talking. This was God.

I love the way Acts 4:13 puts it: "Observing the boldness of Peter and John and realizing them to be uneducated and untrained men, they were amazed and knew that they had been with Jesus."

This is our kingdom calling in a nutshell. But how in the world are people like you and me supposed to accomplish it? Through the power of the Holy Spirit.

The Father wants to empower you for kingdom activity so that the people in your sphere of influence will recognize that you have been with Jesus. God doesn't want you to do kingdom work *for him*. He wants you to allow him to do kingdom work *through you*.

We all know the verse, "I am able to do all things through Him who strengthens me" (Phil. 4:13). But do we really believe it? Are we sure this promise applies to us?

Only if we're convinced that "thine is the power."

THINE IS THE GLORY

Glory is one of my favorite words—a beautiful and powerful biblical concept that attempts to describe God's manifest presence, the way he reveals his splendorous reality to us. In the Old Testament, God displayed his glory through spectacular expressions like the burning bush, the pillar of fire and cloud, even the smoke that filled the temple of Solomon on its dedication day.

In the New Testament, however, we see God showing mankind his glory in a new way: "The Word became flesh and took up residence among us. We observed His glory, the glory as the only Son from the Father, full of grace and truth" (John 1:14). Jesus was God's glory in person, and he displayed this glory by doing things like turning water into wine and raising Lazarus from the dead.

But nowhere was God's glory more evident, perhaps, than when his Son approached the cross, praying to the Father in utter abandonment and radical obedience, "I have glorified You on the earth by completing the work You gave Me to do. Now, Father, glorify Me in Your presence with that glory I had with You before the world existed" (John 17:4–5).

Imagine what glory that must have been!

And yet I can tell you how a person like you or me can get a taste of that glory. Jesus said that he had been "glorified" in his disciples (John 17:10)—both those who were with him then and those of us who are with him now. As he said to the Father, "I have given them the glory that You have given to Me" (John 17:22).

His glory dwells in us. But the only way to experience it . . . is to let it shine through us.

The Father had sent the Son into the world on a redemptive mission—to manifest his glory. And "just as You sent Me into the world," Jesus said, "I also have sent them into the world" (John 17:18)—to testify to the reality of our relationship with him, to be an ambassador of his kingdom, to show forth the Father's glory.

Don't try to hold it in. You can only enjoy it as it's coming out.

This truth ought to make every day a breathless wonder—every personal encounter, every worship opportunity, every waking hour. *God wants to manifest his glory in your life all day long to advance his kingdom.* Just imagine what that might look like on you this afternoon or tomorrow morning or before the weekend's out.

Have you ever thought about yourself as radiating God's glory? This is why God's plan for redeeming the world requires people who will display his character through their behavior, advance his kingdom with every fiber of their being, and live by every word he speaks. We are his movable possessions, a priestly nation, a holy people by design and by redemption.

Life is not about our glory. It's about *his* glory bursting forth through us. Where God's people are, his glory shines through them, illuminating a world held captive to the thick darkness of sin.

Yes, God's kingdom, power, and glory—even though they are alive and active within us—get some stiff and vocal competition from *our* kingdom, *our* power, and *our* glory. But that's why "thine" is such an important word to remember from the Lord's Prayer.

"Thine" is the kingdom, the power, and the glory . . . and the purpose for kingdom people.

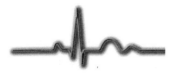

- How can praying "thine is the kingdom" affect your daily life?
- Do you more often feel powerful or powerless? What kind of power would you like to have? How would you use it?
- Have you ever seen God's glory in someone? Has anyone ever seen God's glory in you?

Chapter 23

CLEARED FOR TAKEOFF

For if you forgive people their wrongdoing,
your heavenly Father will forgive you as well.
But if you don't forgive people, your Father
will not forgive your wrongdoing.

MATTHEW 6:14–15

DO YOU FIND IT CURIOUS that right after Jesus offered the Lord's Prayer, he immediately started talking about forgiveness? Why would that be?

In the prayer itself, he had framed this line: "Forgive us our debts, as we also have forgiven our debtors" (Matt. 6:12). I suppose he may have noticed on his disciples' faces the impact this statement had created—a sort of explosion in their wills. It certainly has that kind of effect on us, even from *this* distance. Do we honestly want God to forgive us in the same stingy way we often distribute our forgiveness to others?

It truly is a chilling thought.

Forgiveness, however, is at the heart of kingdom relationships. To begin with, we cannot become kingdom people at all without first experiencing God's forgiveness. Remember that Jesus' inaugural kingdom message began with the word "repent."

But throughout our lives this recognition of both God's holiness and our own sinfulness continues to drive us into prayer, seeking our Father's forgiveness. As kingdom children, we place so much value on the intimacy we enjoy with our Dad, we can't allow anything to hinder our relationship—even for a brief moment. We need forgiveness and we know it. So we go to our Father in prayer.

Have you ever thought, though, that prayer is really a family affair—not just conversation between Father and child but also a way of reminding ourselves that we are responsible members of the family of God, that we are in community with one another.

Look at it this way. In all of the statements of request found in the Lord's Prayer, each of the pronouns Jesus used are plural:

- "Give *us* today *our* daily bread."
- "Do not bring *us* into temptation."
- "Deliver *us* from the evil one."

We don't just pray for ourselves. We pray for one another.

And the request for forgiveness is no different. "Forgive *us our* debts, as *we* also have forgiven *our* debtors."

So for the same reason that I cannot pray for my own "daily bread" while remaining unconcerned for my brother's *lack* of bread, I cannot receive God's forgiveness for myself without being prepared to dispense an equal portion to others. Forgiveness must go both ways in our lives, or we're not going anywhere in the kingdom.

Jesus knew, of course, how difficult this would be to put into practice. I believe this is one of the reasons he so boldly underlined this matter of forgiveness in the Sermon on the Mount.

He also knew that when we forgive others, we show ourselves to be most like our Father, who is "a forgiving God, gracious and compassionate, slow to anger and rich in faithful love" (Neh. 9:17b).

Perhaps more than anything, though, Jesus knew that unforgiveness would choke out our witness and make us ineffective as kingdom people. The weight of even one, little, unforgiving grudge is enough to keep us chained down and immobilized in guilt, bitterness, and hypocrisy. When we don't forgive, our faith can't get off the ground.

But when forgiveness is not just coming *to* us but is also flowing *through* us, we are free to fly. We are prepared to soar into the blue sky of God's everyday opportunity.

We are cleared for kingdom takeoff.

A GOSPEL OF FORGIVENESS

As you study the life of Jesus, you discover that one of the main things about him that most disturbed the religious authorities of his day was his claim of being able to forgive sins—and his willingness to do it so freely.

On one occasion, you remember, when a few friends had brought a paralytic to see Jesus, he said to the crippled man—before even addressing his physical problem: "Have courage, son, your sins are forgiven" (Matt. 9:2). This bold statement certainly startled everyone, but it *really* rattled the cage of the local scribes. "He's blaspheming!" they whispered among themselves. But Jesus confounded them with a simple question: "Which is easier: to say, 'Your sins are forgiven,' or to say, 'Get up and walk'?" (v. 5). Jesus' miracle power proved that he had both the authority and the desire to forgive sins. And although this caused some to give glory to God—the way genuine kingdom activity always will—it drove some of them crazy.

It always does.

Another time a Pharisee named Simon invited Jesus to dinner (Luke 7:36–50). His comfortable banquet was interrupted, though, when a certain woman of the city crashed the party. She stood behind Jesus, flooding his feet with her tears and wiping them with her hair. Simon was perplexed. "This man, if He were a prophet, would know who and what kind of woman this is who is touching Him—that she's a sinner!" (v. 39). But turning to the woman, Jesus simply said, "Your sins are forgiven." And those reclining at the table could only mutter to one another, "Who is this man who even forgives sins?" (vv. 48–49).

Even as Jesus was celebrating Passover with his disciples, preparing them for his impending death, he took the cup of wine and declared: "This is My blood of the covenant, which is shed for many for the forgiveness of sins" (Matt. 26:28). This solemn declaration, rich in Old Testament imagery, indicated that the sacrificial death of Jesus would inaugurate a new relationship between God and his people. As the Old Testament prophets had foreseen, God was raising up a new covenant community—no longer defined by national identity but by redemptive relationship.

The kingdom was being born in forgiveness.

Jesus went to the cross dispensing this forgiveness. Luke recorded that among the final few words Jesus spoke before dying were the illogical lines of this agonizing prayer: "Father, forgive

them, because they do not know what they are doing"
(Luke 23:34).

His was a liberating gospel of forgiveness.

BETWEEN US AND GOD

So those of us who are kingdom children—born in forgiveness and raised on God's grace—cannot survive for long in a sinful state, dragging behind us that awful, nagging sense of
separation. Sin keeps us from our deepest need—fellowship with
the Father. And therefore, we don't want even a moment to pass
by with his face blurred or his presence obscured.

And that's exactly what happens when we keep sin alive in our
hearts. The psalmist declared, "If I had been aware of malice in my
heart, the Lord would not have listened" (Ps. 66:18). Sin disrupts
the intimate family communion between us and our Dad.

And we don't want any part of it.

If we ever cease to feel this way, there are probably two reasons
to blame:

1. *We've forgotten the enormous cost of our forgiveness.*
Whenever we treat the confession of our sins lightly, it's usually
because we've failed to remember that our forgiveness required
the sacrificial death of Christ.

2. *We've forgotten that our sin is directed at God alone.* You
remember that David took another man's wife and then sent her
husband to the front line of battle to be killed. He had obviously
sinned against two specific individuals. Yet he declared to God,
"Against You—You alone—I have sinned and done this evil in
Your sight. So You are right when You pass sentence; You are

blameless when You judge" (Ps. 51:4). Joseph, when tempted by Potiphar's wife, responded with the same kind of understanding. Sure, he was genuinely concerned about not breaking the trust of his employer, the husband of his seducer. But beyond that, he saw a much larger issue: "How could I do such a great evil and sin against God?" (Gen. 39:9).

Seeking the kingdom and clinging to sin are incompatible.

BETWEEN US AND OTHERS

But forgiveness is not simply a matter between God and us. To experience his forgiveness in all its glory, we must also make it a matter between us and others.

Again, let me direct you to the plural pronouns of the Lord's Prayer. Kingdom citizens are part of a larger family, and therefore sin is never an isolated occurrence. Our sins hurt others. Their sins hurt us. And the sin of unforgiveness only makes things worse. Whenever someone has sinned against us, we should be ready to forgive . . . just the way God has forgiven us.

"For if you forgive people their wrongdoing, your heavenly Father will forgive you as well. But if you don't forgive people, your Father will not forgive your wrongdoing" (Matt. 6:14–15).

This doesn't mean, now, that our willingness to offer forgiveness to others *enables* God to forgive us. Some have misunderstood this, but the entire witness of Scripture is clear on the matter. We can do nothing to earn his forgiveness (Rom. 5:6–8). Grace flows from the character of God. He applied his forgiveness to us while we were still sinners, enemies in full rebellion. It's not like he's waiting around for us to forgive others, and then if we don't, our forgiveness might be yanked or withheld. We didn't earn it to begin with; we can't lose it in the end.

So when we refuse to forgive others, it doesn't thwart God's ability to forgive, *but it does block our capacity to receive his forgiveness freely offered.*

The issue here is clear: forgiveness is not a one-way street. If we're going to be able to enjoy his blessing of forgiveness—like all the rest of God's gifts—we must be willing to bestow it on others.

Peter thought he had a handle on this the day he asked Jesus, "Lord, how many times could my brother sin against me and I forgive him? As many as seven times?" (Matt. 18:21). This was pretty noble and generous of Peter, seeing as how the rabbis considered three times to be quite sufficient.

Jesus answered him with a kingdom parable, the story of a king whose servant owed him "ten thousand talents." No one's absolutely certain how much money that was, but most say the amount was around $10 million in silver. We do know for sure, at least, that a "talent" was the highest unit of the day's currency, and we also know that "ten thousand" was the largest Greek numeral.

Do you remember how as a child you would make up strange names for huge amounts of money? You'd say something like, "When I grow up, I'm going to earn a trillion-zillion dollars!" The effect here is the same. The number is so large, repayment is clearly impossible.

But the servant didn't seem to grasp the enormity of his debt. If he had, he wouldn't have stalled for more time. He wouldn't have continued to promise that he'd eventually pay everything back (v. 26). Still, rather than offering him patience, the king granted him forgiveness of all the debt. All trillion-zillion dollars of it.

We all know where Jesus is going with this.

We remember how the pardoned slave left the king's presence and, instead of spreading the wealth of his newfound forgiveness, hunted down a fellow slave who owed him "a hundred denarii." Scholars figure this amount to be about ten dollars. And unbelievably—or is it really all that hard to believe?—the man who had been forgiven such a colossal amount of money had no mercy on the one who owed him so little in comparison.

No, Peter, don't just forgive *seven* times, "but seventy times seven" (v. 22). A *trillion-zillion* times seven. The same way God has forgiven you.

When we comprehend the enormity of the debt we've been forgiven, we will never hold back forgiveness—even over issues that seem so huge and impossible to work around.

I have seen families split over issues of unforgiveness. I've seen the ministry of entire churches sacrificed over hurt feelings and angry words. Somewhere along the way, someone refused to forgive and forget. And the dark shadow of sin fell across everybody.

Jesus' concern for the purity and unity of his kingdom community was so intense that he instructed his worshippers to leave their gifts at the altar—interrupting their worship—and to go to their brother to seek reconciliation with him (Matt. 5:23–24). What would happen if we took this command seriously? How many of us would have to make a side trip on the way to church this Sunday?

Why don't we? Maybe we should.

When we read the Bible, we like it when our personal pronouns are the subject of the sentence—when *we* are "heirs according to the promise" (Gal. 3:29)—when *we* are "protected by God's power" (1 Pet. 1:5)—when *we* are "called God's children" (1 John 3:1). In the Lord's Prayer, though, *we* are the subject of the sentence only one time: when *we* are given the responsibility to forgive those who have sinned against us.

How do we go about this? After all, a grudge is sometimes just too precious to give up! Sometimes a past hurt can be too deep in memory, too painful even to think about, caked with complications. The key question you must ask yourself, though, is this: "Will I choose to forgive others as the Father has forgiven me?"

Here are a few practical steps:

1. Remember the debt you have been forgiven.
2. Ask the Holy Spirit to enable you to forgive.
3. Remember the importance of the kingdom community to your Father.
4. Release the other person in the same manner you have been released by God.
5. Begin to pray for God to bless the person you need to forgive.
6. Begin to do loving things for the person who injured you.
7. Then initiate the peacemaking visit. Go to the person and acknowledge your desire for restored fellowship.

It may not heal everything. But where bitterness is a teeming swamp of misery, distrust, and heartbreak, forgiveness is a clear step of obedience, love, and gratitude.

And it's a step we all have to take before we can fly.

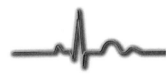

- If God forgives you as you forgive others, will your acts of forgiveness be adequate to cover your need to be forgiven?
- Which is greater in your life, to be truly forgiven for everything you've ever done wrong or to be healed physically? Are either/both miracles? If they are miracles, how do they make you want to respond to God? To others?
- Do you have a human relationship that needs to be mended in order to have a better relationship with God?
- Are there sins in your life that are affecting your relationship with God? Will you repent, seek forgiveness, and rid yourself of the wrongdoing?

Chapter 24

THE WORRY-LESS LIFE

**But seek first the kingdom of God and His righteousness,
and all these things will be provided for you.**

MATTHEW 6:33

WHEN WE SOLD our first house, we gave the buyers a second loan on it. And soon after we moved to Norfolk, they in turn sold the house. Suddenly we had a little extra money we hadn't anticipated having.

We wanted to be responsible stewards of this unexpected windfall, so I asked one of the men at our church who worked with investments to advise me. He began by asking me what our plans for the money were, what we hoped to achieve as a result of our investing. Without thinking, I responded that we wanted a little financial security. I'll never forget what he said in return: "Preacher, of all people, you should know there's no security in money!"

Ouch. Good point.

He went on to explain, of course, that no financial venture was 100 percent sure. Every investment vehicle comes with its own inherent risks.

I knew him well enough to know that what he really meant by his first statement had a much broader reach. He wasn't just commenting about the delicate mix of stocks and bonds that can prove risky in people's lives. He was saying that all of our earthly possessions are temporary at best. All of them. Always.

We all know that. Don't we?

As Jesus continued his Sermon on the Mount, he too began to discuss the issue of possessions in the lives of kingdom people. Unlike some preachers, he wasn't afraid to talk about money and stewardship. In fact, Jesus actually had more to say about money than he did heaven or hell. He knew—yes—that money, stuff, and things can be real blessings in the believer's life. They have the potential to flow through us and advance God's kingdom activity on earth.

But they also have the power to steal our hearts.

And this is one worry kingdom people can live without.

TREASURE IN HEAVEN

Jesus spoke of two possible places we could store our treasure—on earth or in heaven. As believers, we know that heaven's vault provides the greatest level of safety and security for our possessions. We understand that everything will last longer in there than it will on earth. Since we're familiar with the damage that "moths" and "rust" and "thieves" can have on our things (Matt. 6:19), and since we're confident that this earth is destined to pass away, we see the futility of hoarding up material worth while we're here. Such an investment strategy is the equivalent of buying a company's stock the day after they've declared bankruptcy. Not a very good deal!

To summarize, we know you can't take it with you. We understand that.

But what does Jesus mean when he talks about storing up "treasures in heaven"? (v. 20). How do we do that?

I believe there's way more than one answer to this question. But here are a few:

In Matthew 19, Jesus told the rich young ruler that *he* could have "treasure in heaven" by selling his belongings and giving the proceeds to the poor (v. 21). So we know from this and many other Bible passages that the giving of our money to the needy is one good way to make a heavenly investment.

But it's not the only way. Paul counseled Timothy to teach the rich "not to be arrogant or to set their hope on the uncertainty of wealth, but on God, who richly provides us with all things to enjoy. Instruct them," Paul said, "to do good, to be rich in good works, to be generous, willing to share, storing up for themselves a good foundation for the age to come, so that they may take hold of the life that is real" (1 Tim. 6:17–19). To obey God in every aspect of our lives and purposefully to use the blessings of God to do "good works" in the lives of others are both eternal transactions.

Here's another way. We believe God's mission from the beginning of time has been to draw people to himself from every tribe, tongue, and nation. Obviously, then, giving our money to missions through our local churches—or even giving up our vacation time to take an active part in missions opportunities ourselves—should be part of our strategy for storing "treasures in heaven."

Do you see the connection here, though? We store treasure in heaven by giving to needy *people,* by doing good works for other *people,* by supporting missions causes that take the gospel to unsaved *people.*

Look around you. What in your world is eternal? Your diploma? Your home entertainment system? Your week at the beach every summer?

The only thing that's truly eternal around you and me today is people—human beings whose souls will live on after they die. Some will be redeemed and will live forever. Some will be lost and will face God's righteous judgment. But putting our energies into serving, helping, loving, encouraging, and supporting other people is how *kingdom* people invest in eternity.

Our money is God's money, and it's intended to be used to advance his kingdom. But storing "treasure in heaven" is so much more than just putting money in an offering plate. It's about investing in our children rather than loading them up with nothing but gifts and gadgets. It's about investing in our families rather than filling all our free time with pleasure. It's about investing in our neighbors rather than sinking all our time and money into the lawn and the landscaping.

It's not wrong to possess things, but we can't let things possess us. Money itself doesn't pose a threat to the kingdom person. But those who love it will always struggle when called upon to share it.

Remember the rich fool in Jesus' parable? The one who decided to build bigger barns to hoard his surplus? His problem wasn't that he had too much money. He just had the wrong priorities and perspectives on money.

1. *He had an "I" problem.* He talked about "my crops," "my barns," "my grain," "my goods," "my soul." He failed to understand that everything he owned was on temporary loan from the Father.

2. *He had a storage mentality.* The only thing he knew to do with the profit from a good year's crop was to build a bigger place to put it. He had no vision, no desire to use it and invest it, just to "store" it. As I've said before, God's blessings are meant to be conveyed, not consumed.

3. *He had an earthly end.* He spent the last day of his life preparing for a long, earthly future, without giving any thought to his preparation for eternity. From a heavenly perspective, then, this made him exactly what Jesus called him—a "fool!"

And when we put stock in our "treasures on earth," we look every bit as foolish as this guy did. We end up looking like everybody else, and our kingdom witness loses its punch and power.

ONE OR THE OTHER

A kingdom person having money and nice things is not a contradiction in terms. But "no one can be a slave of two masters," as Jesus said. "You cannot be slaves of God and of money" (Matt. 6:24).

In first-century culture a slave owner could actually rent out one of his servants to another taskmaster. Such an arrangement always put the servant in a bind. What if the two men gave conflicting orders? How was he supposed to respond? Who was he supposed to listen to? Perhaps you've been in a situation like this at work, with two supervisors telling you to do two different things, disagreeing about how you should do your job. Frustrating, isn't it?

Jesus was right. It makes you "hate one and love the other, or be devoted to one and despise the other" (v. 24). "Hate" may come across a little strong to us, but the idea of *hating* was a Hebrew idiom that meant "to love less" or "to be indifferent toward" (Deut. 21:15; Luke 14:26). No matter how hard the slave tried, one master would always be slighted.

But the kingdom person never wants to put himself in a position where he might choose to slight his king!

This is why we cannot be "slaves of God and of money." When money becomes our master, it can cause us to compromise our integrity, to use people, and to ignore God. Paul warned that "those who want to be rich fall into temptation, a trap, and many foolish and harmful desires, which plunge people into ruin and destruction" (1 Tim. 6:9). Money can make us deaf, dumb, and blind to the things of God. It can alter our spiritual judgment and harden the arteries of compassionate generosity.

How do we claim victory in this area of our lives? We begin by acknowledging that we possess nothing. We determine that our role in regard to money is merely to be a responsible steward of it. We look for opportunities to invest in kingdom activity through our church, our denomination, and other missions organizations that are advancing God's kingdom. We become involved personally and financially with relief organizations in our own communities.

We let the kingdom control our checkbook.

THE END OF ANXIETY

And guess what God does as a result of our faithfulness?

He promises to take the worry out of life.

Do you think it's possible to live without anxiety? Would you like to do so? Five times in the ten verses, Matthew 6:25–34, Jesus used the word *worry*. And in all three of these instances, he spoke

it as a command: "Don't worry." He wasn't merely making a suggestion or trying to calm people down. This was an order!
"Worry," he was saying, should be banned from the kingdom
person's heart.

Why is it wrong for kingdom people to be fraught with worry?

1. *Worry is futile and counterproductive.* Jesus pointedly asked
whether anxiety could add even a short time to our life spans
(v. 27). In truth, doctors tell us that anxiety will most likely *shorten*
our lifetimes.

2. *Worry indicates a lack of understanding.* The nature and
character of our Father is to feed the songbirds and water the
wildflowers. "Aren't you worth more than they?" (v. 26). To fail to
trust God is to doubt who he is.

3. *Worry demonstrates a lack of faith.* Jesus said it takes a person "of little faith" to worry about his needs being met (v. 30).
Guess what? That's what everyone else will think, too. So what
impact does anxiety have on our kingdom witness?

4. *Worry is a pagan response to life.* Of all the arguments
against anxiety, this one should perhaps stun us the most. If worry
is the pattern that comes most naturally to everyone (v. 32), why
would we want to be known for being like the average unbeliever?
As kingdom people, there should be numerous things about us
that can only be explained by the presence of the Holy Spirit
within us. And freedom from worry is one of them.

Jesus wasn't suggesting, of course, that we embrace the "don't
worry, be happy" philosophy of life made popular by the movie
The Lion King. The kind of faith he was talking about is not a
weak, irresponsible, "who cares" attitude toward the future.
Nowhere in the Sermon on the Mount does Jesus ever indicate

that his followers should view life with passive indifference or that they should avoid work and ignore planning for the future.

Kingdom trust is not wimpy, wishful thinking. It is a courageous choice to live up to our privilege. It is a deliberate decision to live in kingdom reality. It is an active trust in an all-sufficient God.

Here are three basic steps to overcoming anxiety:

1. *Get your priorities straight.* Jesus painted this so simply: "Seek first the kingdom of God and His righteousness, and all these things will be provided for you" (Matt. 6:33). This is not a get-rich scheme but a promise of heavenly blessing. When we focus on the things that matter most to God, he takes care of the rest.

2. *Rely on the character of your Father.* He knows what we need and is already supplying it. We can rest in who he is and be sure we're on his mind.

3. *Pray rather than worry.* "Don't worry about anything, but in everything, through prayer and petition with thanksgiving, let your requests be made known to God" (Phil. 4:6). Turn your worry lines into prayer lyrics.

Some people say that kingdom living just gives us a lot more we have to do.

I say it just gives us a lot less to worry about.

- What do you worry about?
- Where do you seek security?
- How does your level of anxiety reflect where you put your trust?

Chapter 25

A CALL
TO COMMUNITY

**Therefore, whatever you want others to do for you,
do also the same for them—this is the Law and the Prophets.**

MATTHEW 7:12

THROUGHOUT THE COURSE of this book, we've seen that the kingdom has always existed in the heart of God. We've also seen that it continues to exist right now in real time. And we've seen that the kingdom has a future dimension, as well.

The kingdom has been, the kingdom is here, and the kingdom is coming. All of these statements are true.

The table of contents for this book has been set up to express this kingdom continuum. But the reason for this particular section, "The Kingdom Lives," has been to show that the kingdom we experience today is not just some mysterious concept or theory. It is a living reality. It is an active organism, filled with triumphs and trials and every-other-Tuesdays. Yes, the kingdom *lives*.

But we need to be sure we define this properly. We've been frequently reminded through our look at the Sermon on the Mount that the Christian life is corporate in nature. Jesus vividly underlined this when he framed our prayer requests in plural pronouns. He stated it bluntly in his command that we forgive others, as well as in his instructions to the would-be worshipper to leave his gift at the altar and be reconciled with his brother. He made clear in his warning about storing up treasures for ourselves rather than investing his blessings in the lives of others.

The kingdom lives only in community.

In the final third of the Sermon on the Mount—Matthew 7—Jesus spent much of his time teaching his disciples the responsibility they should feel for one another, their need to empty themselves of rights and privileges in order to protect the hearts of their brothers and sisters.

For many people today, church has become a casual option. Even among those who attend regularly, many of them merely come for the services and ministries that appeal to their personal tastes and needs. It's not uncommon to see individuals and families flit from one church to another in the same town, staying just long enough for the new to wear off, until the hard work of living in harmony with one another starts getting personal and unpleasant. To many modern-day Christians, community is fine as long as it's fun and feels good and fits into their schedule.

This isn't the kind of community Jesus was talking about. The kingdom community is a unity of people brought together under the banner of God's redemptive mercy and love. It's not always an easy mix of personalities and backgrounds. The challenges of getting along and remaining loyal to one another can be enough to prompt many a surrender and letter of resignation.

But the kingdom in community is the visible picture of God's grace in the world. Through the collective witness of our shared faith, we do more to showcase God's glory than all of our personal acts and accolades could achieve in a lifetime.

To people called into community and knit together in king-dom purpose, the work may be tough and the devil's opposition ferocious. But we are the family of God.

And we are here, together, to stay.

Thankfully, Jesus shared with us a few things we'd need to know going in—about not being critical of one another, about putting others first, about protecting our brothers' and sisters' hearts, and about living with one another in mind.

TAKE IT EASY

"Do not judge, so that you won't be judged" (Matt. 7:1). Our society may not know much about the Bible, but it loves to quote this verse. They take it to mean that we have no right to exercise any discernment in distinguishing right from wrong or to have a principled opinion about another person's behavior. They main-tain that we're to accept anything and everything uncritically, without blinking an eye or raising a question.

That is not what this verse is saying.

On the contrary, we are commanded to "test" all forms of teach-ing to determine "what is good" (1 Thess. 5:21), and not to "believe every spirit" but to reject false doctrine (1 John 4:1). God has given us a standard to judge between truth and error, and he expects us to use it. The Bible also gives us a description of "how people ought to act in God's household, which is the church of the living God" (1 Tim. 3:15), and we as a kingdom community may often have need to rebuke our brothers over their sin (Matt. 18:15–17).

The issue in this "do not judge" verse is not whether we can hold one another accountable. The activity Jesus is condemning is the petty faultfinding whose only purpose is to hurt and put down.

The Pharisees in their false righteousness had no qualms about belittling others in order to make themselves look holy by comparison. This pharisaic attitude still invades the church today—with similarly devastating results. Like few others, this sin ruptures fellowship in the community. And instead of making us look big by pointing out the faults of others, it actually makes us look ridiculously narrow and self-serving.

Any time we're tempted to make ourselves appear holier by climbing over another's reputation, we should heed the warning of Jesus: "For with the judgment you use, you will be judged, and with the measure you use, it will be measured to you" (Matt. 7:2).

On one level this is simply a statement of consequence. It means we'll usually receive from others exactly what we dish out. If we tend to be critical and judgmental of our brothers and sisters, we can expect the same kind of treatment in return. Since those who are the most adept at passing out judgment are often the most sensitive when they receive a dose of their own medicine themselves, this warning is particularly appropriate. *Think before you speak,* Jesus is saying. Your words could come back to haunt you.

But the issue here is much greater than this. The passive tense of the verb in Matthew 7:2 suggests that *God himself* will judge those who treat others in a harsh, unforgiving manner. People who are quick to cut down will soon find that they have more than just *other people* to contend with. They'll find themselves contending with Almighty God.

And no kingdom person wants to put himself in that position.

Jesus explained this problem and its solution by using an illustration drawn from the carpenter's workshop—the analogy between having a "speck" or a "log" in our eyes (vv. 3–5). This idea is certainly graphic and slightly grotesque, but it clearly communicates two points:

1. *We naturally tend to exaggerate.* We often inflate the faults of others while at the same time underestimating our own.

2. *The best judges judge themselves first.* Before we can really be of much use in dealing with the "speck" in our brother's eye, we must be willing to deal honestly with our own sins. This doesn't mean we have to be perfect before we can help someone else face the sin in his life. But it does mean we should be just as willing for our own lives to be inspected as we are to examine others.

We should no more avoid self-examination than an athlete would go into competition without first checking every piece of equipment, every potential point of weakness, every joint and muscle. When we're serious about examining ourselves thoroughly and biblically, then our purpose and passion in confronting others will be to build them up, not to tear them down. Unlike the Pharisees, who judged others to make *themselves* look good, the kingdom person judges himself to help *others* look good.

Have you ever had someone attempt to help you remove something from your eye? If so, you can readily understand the amount of gentleness and tenderness that's required. When we minister to one another in the Christian community, we must do so only after careful introspection to make sure our own motives are pure. Then we can proceed with appropriate care and humility.

Paul summarized this principle well in Galatians 6:1: "Brothers, if someone is caught in any wrongdoing, you who are spiritual should restore such a person with a gentle spirit, watching out for yourselves so you won't be tempted also."

"Do not judge"? That's right. We're not to be hypercritical and speak ugly of others behind their backs. But "speck" removal is not against the rules of the kingdom community. In fact, we can and must assist one another in dealing with sin.

It's part of being a responsible kingdom citizen.

THE GOLDEN RULE

The word "therefore" that begins Matthew 7:12 almost seems to link this verse to the whole teaching of the Sermon of the Mount. Everything Jesus had said up until now—about showing mercy and seeking peace, about surpassing the righteousness of the Pharisees, about maintaining pure and generous motives in the giving of our money—all of these can be summarized in this one simple statement.

"Whatever you want others to do for you, do also the same for them."

We find examples of similar statements in both contemporary Jewish and secular literature, but only from the lips of Jesus do we hear these words spoken in a positive, proactive manner. Jesus expects kingdom citizens to take the initiative in doing good to others. If we want people to love us, we should start the ball rolling by loving them first. If we want people to forgive us, then we must initiate and model forgiveness.

I'm not suggesting for a minute that this is the sum total of truth or a means of salvation. In fact, this is an impossible ethic for anyone who has not entered the kingdom of God through faith in Jesus Christ.

But the life of the kingdom citizen—and the reputation of the kingdom community—should be marked by this "golden rule" because we alone possess the ability and character to obey it. The Holy Spirit, given to us through the new birth, has genetically encoded greater righteousness in us.

It should be what our family is known for.

THE REAL THING

Basically, kingdom people are just called to be genuine, to embody the name and character of our Father. Unless this quality is ingrained inside us, life in the community will always be riddled with pettiness, strife, and distrust. Unless our purposes are consistent with embracing God's mission and obeying his Word, our relationships with one another will remain in a constant state of collision.

Our confession of faith cannot be merely words alone. Jesus said, "Not everyone who says to Me, 'Lord, Lord!' will enter the kingdom of heaven, but the one who does the will of My Father in heaven" (v. 21). His repetition of the word *Lord* in this verse indicates an emphatic profession of faith. There's no suggestion that the person making the statement is insincere. The problem is, he is self-deceived.

We need more than a statement of Christian faith. We need Christian obedience—not to save us but to identify us, not to make us feel prideful but to assure us that the Word is sinking in, that our confession is true. The kingdom citizen will hear the King's words and obey them, and in doing so he will honor his Lord and give credence to his faith.

Oh, how our churches need this kind of obedience and biblical framework! Only in knowing the Word can we understand our kingdom calling and live it with abandon. Only in understanding the Scriptures can we protect our communities from "false prophets" and teachings that come to us "in sheep's clothing, but inwardly are ravaging wolves" (v. 15).

We don't need more religious activity for activity's sake, but we desperately need a genuine, personal relationship with Jesus Christ, which in turn will cause us to obey him out of love and not duty.

"On that day"—a reference to the final judgment—"many will say to Me, 'Lord, Lord, didn't we prophesy in Your name, drive out demons in Your name, and do many miracles in Your name?' Then I will announce to them, 'I never knew you!'" (vv. 22–23). There will be no pretense when we encounter the resurrected King. Only those whose confession and obedience line up— whose "fruit" is in keeping with the fruit of their lips (v. 20)—will enter into the kingdom prepared for them by the Father.

But rather than striking us with fear and dread, this should enliven us to consume ourselves in loving our King, to invest ourselves completely in his kingdom work, to place our arms in genuine love around the shoulders of our brothers and sisters—and serve the Lord together in unity and power.

The kingdom rules and reigns in the hearts of individual believers. But the kingdom only lives and thrives as his people come together in community.

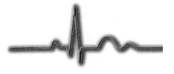

- What evidence do you see that the concept of "community" has changed?
- What does community mean to you?
- Where do you find community

SECTION 6

His Kingdom Never Ends

Chapter 26

GATE CRASHERS

**On this rock I will build My church,
and the forces of Hades will not overpower it.
I will give you the keys of the kingdom of heaven.**

MATTHEW 16:18–19

IT WAS 1991. We were at war. And a large number of members from our church in Norfolk had been dispatched to the Persian Gulf for Operation Desert Storm.

These were turbulent days for those in our naval community, and we wanted to be sure we were ready to minister to them. Once war was officially declared, I remember gathering my staff to discuss how we should respond to the open doors for evangelism this crisis would create, to think through the many ways we would need to nurture and care for our military families, and to seek God's wisdom and direction.

I also knew that the sermon I was preparing for the following Sunday morning was critical. Many would be coming to hear what God's people had to say about the outbreak of hostilities, wanting a word from the Lord to help put them at peace and give them good reason for hope and trust. So during our time together as a staff, I asked them how they thought I could best minister from the pulpit that Sunday.

One of them noticed that I was scheduled to preach on this passage from Matthew 16: "On this rock I will build My church, and the forces of Hades will not overpower it." I must confess I was having some reservations about the appropriateness of this text, which I had chosen months earlier, long before the recent events had unfolded. I'll never forget what my friend Dick Baker said. "Dr. Hemphill, I've heard you preach on this text before. When you talk about this, don't you say that the decisions made in the life of the church have greater eternal significance than any decision made in the halls of Washington, D.C.?" I admitted that this would definitely be part of the message. "If you believe that," he said, "then why would you think of changing it? That is precisely what we need to hear!"

Truly, the power of God is always at work in his church, in his kingdom people—in times of rising fear and anxiety—in every situation, no matter how dire or distressing.

Yes, this is precisely what we need to hear! It's what Jesus knew his followers needed to hear at this particular point in their lives. And it's still what we need to hear today.

Truly, this is one of the most profound and remarkable passages of Matthew's Gospel. It illuminates much of what he had already reported in his account of Christ's life, and it prepares us for what's to come. The setting alone is worth noting. Here was the King of the universe, ministering in the idolatrous city of Caesarea Philippi—the very place where Herod the Great had built a temple of white marble to Caesar Augustus—announcing to his disciples the two prongs of his incredible mission:

- He was going to be killed.
- And he was going to conquer.

This is the divine paradox. Yes, he was about to "suffer many things"—even a wicked crucifixion at the hands of the "elders, chief priests, and scribes." His death, however, would not be the end but a glorious beginning, for he would "be raised the third day" (v. 21).

And rising with him—established upon his death sentence and ignited by his resurrection—would be his church. In breaking the curse of sin and death, Jesus would empower this new, messianic community to fulfill his commission: making disciples of all the nations (Matt. 28:19–20).

We are living in these days—standing on the walls, pounding on the gates, marching with a head of steam and a wave of confidence—as his kingdom comes.

ON THIS ROCK

Two things make this passage so powerful. One is the confession of Peter, articulating what Matthew had referred to editorially throughout his Gospel, but which no one had actually said out loud before: "You are the Messiah, the Son of the living God!" (v. 16).

Matthew alone recorded the second half of Peter's statement. This phrase—"the Son of the living God"—took the Messiah's role far beyond any nationalistic interpretation. It declared that Jesus had a special relationship with the Father, that he was more than the Savior of one group but the Savior of all. We can almost imagine Jesus saying, "My role was to show you the Father through my life and words, and I have succeeded. You have recognized the family resemblance."

In order for us to hear Peter's confession with the raw power of its first-century setting, we must remember that these disciples were Hebrew to the core. They knew from what the prophets said, they knew from their upbringing and religious nostalgia, that a Messiah was coming one day. But to have this reality revealed to them by God (v. 17), to actually see this Messiah standing within an arm's length, where they could touch him and ask him questions and recognize the inflections in his voice—this was unbelievable! It was the dawning of a new day, a new era—the day of redemption! The One described by Isaiah as both a Servant and King was here, in the flesh!

Can you imagine the unbridled excitement and anticipation?

Then, responding to the lightning strike of Peter's bold assertion, Jesus added the second punch: "On this rock I will build My church, and the forces of Hades will not overpower it" (v. 18).

Throughout the Old Testament, *rock* was a visual symbol of God (Deut. 32:4; Ps. 18:2, 31). And here we see the Rock in human form—Jesus of Nazareth, "the Son of the living God"—preparing to "build" something more powerful, alive, and indestructible than anything the world had ever seen. Jesus himself was going to construct it on his own strong shoulders, equip it with authority, and launch it into human history with both might and a mission.

And with a new twist on an old name: *ecclesia.*

The Greeks used this term to refer to the assembly of its free men in the cities. The Old Testament Scriptures had used a similar term to refer to the "congregation" or "community," which marked Israel as a select, God-governed people.

Now Jesus was transforming this word into a new idea—the church—not *equating* it with the kingdom of God but *initiating* it as his primary instrument for advancing the kingdom. He would entrust it with the timeless message of his redemption and enable it to carry the torch of truth through times of both peace and war, fruitfulness and decay, light and darkness.

He would build it person by person—"living stone" upon "living stone."

And his church would change the world.

FOR WHAT PURPOSE?

The church today is busy doing a lot of things—a lot of *good* things, for the most part. But many churches are stuck in that Sunday-to-Sunday mentality, just surviving from one week to the next, perpetuating themselves through meetings, activities, and long-held traditions.

Surely the church is meant for more than that.

Jesus said his church was designed to assault the "forces of Hades," more familiarly known as the "gates of hell." Gates, in biblical terminology, represent authority and power. The "gates of hell," then, stand for the power of death.

It would be one thing if our King had merely declared *war* on death, if he had simply threatened to remove it from the earth, if he had dared the devil to meet him on the battlefield—and may the best man win. But our King has gone beyond *declaring* war. He has already won the war! He has conquered the enemy by becoming the perfect sacrifice, by bursting from the tomb in glory. And he is leading his church today as he has led it for two thousand years—marching in triumph, proclaiming victory over death.

Death. It's the last and most feared enemy of man. Set loose on the world as a consequence of human sin and held in place by Satan's temporary authority, death casts its long, dark shadow over everyone. But by the power of the resurrected Christ, his church has the authority to rescue the lost from the doomed city of death—a city whose gates are already crumbling in the kingdom's wake—and to usher them into God's new city, where there will be no more death, no more loss, no more pain.

And the gates of hell can do nothing to stop it.

This is the church's mission and privilege.

Wouldn't you love to be part of a church with this kind of calling—a church that's actively at work eradicating death in people's lives, displaying Christ's overcoming power, propelling people throughout your community and around the world to declare that death has lost its "sting"? (see 1 Cor. 15:55).

I have great news for you. Your church already has this calling—an unchanging command from God to *embrace his mission, embody his name, and obey his Word*—to lead the dying to life.

But how?

We'll talk about this more in the next couple of chapters, but Jesus began laying the groundwork for this in these intriguing verses: "I will give you the keys of the kingdom of heaven, and whatever you bind on earth will have been bound in heaven, and whatever you loose on earth will have been loosed in heaven" (v. 19).

Keys, like gates, are also a biblical symbol of authority (Isa. 22:22). And Jesus has given the "keys of the kingdom"—the power and authority of God—to his community, the church. This doesn't make us the porter that decides who gets in but more of a steward who has the authority to show that these keys are real, that they work, that they do indeed lead to life.

The best way I know to describe the "keys" is to think of them as the message of the gospel, which is the only way to be given acceptance into the kingdom. Jesus entrusted these keys into the hands of his apostles, who used them to open the door of faith for both Jew and Gentile alike.

And today these keys are in our hands, placed there by virtue of our relationship with Jesus Christ.

As we who belong to his community of faith proclaim the coming of his kingdom—as we bear witness of his love and grace, as we preach the gospel in faithfulness and truth, as we show others through our words and deeds that this message is indeed for real—and is indeed for *them*—we unlock the gates to life. We put death on notice that we are not merely trying to keep it out; we are taking it on. We are not concerned with desperately defending ourselves from a dying culture but are moving boldly onto death's home ground and declaring to its captives the power of life—*Jesus'* life.

These keys give the church the authority to "bind" and to "loose." These were technical terms in Hebrew thought, referring to the rabbis' pronouncement of certain things and activities as being either permitted or prohibited.

If read one way, this verse almost sounds as if heaven waits to hear what the church has decided to do before God weighs in on a matter, either endorsing or condemning it. We know that can't be right. And in fact, the future perfect verb tense of Matthew 16:19 makes clear that the things we "bind" or "loose" on earth are those things which have *already* "been bound" or "been loosed in heaven."

Jesus has not given his church the authority to tell God what to do but rather the privilege of declaring what God has already established—salvation through Jesus Christ, victory over death, and the eternal reality of his kingdom. After all, we were instructed to pray, "Your kingdom come. Your will be done *on earth as it is in heaven*" (Matt. 6:10).

So while God's people cannot arrogantly guarantee that man's desires will be accomplished in heaven, we can—and must—affirm that God's plans will be accomplished on the earth . . . through his church. Certainly we must be generous with the message of the gospel, which "loosens" repentant hearts to receive the eternal blessings of God. But we must also uphold the truth about man's sinful condition, which "binds" him to the constraints of a human lifetime and results in his ultimate death. As G. Campbell Morgan has stated, "The church is to be, not merely an aggressive force, conquering His enemies, and opening a way out of all prisons; but it is also to interpret to the world the moral standards of life, and to teach men the will of God."[1]

This is not something we can do on our own—individually, by ourselves. God's chosen vehicle for declaring his message and upholding his truth is the *church*—God's kingdom people in community. This is why every kingdom person must *of necessity* identify himself with the church, using his gifts and resources to advance its work as it in turn advances the kingdom.

The King has called.

The dying await.

The gates tremble.

The kingdom comes.

- Do you have a "rock"? What is it?
- If you were asked to make a confession/statement of faith, what would it be?
- How does your confession affect the way you live?

Chapter 27

ACTS ALL OVER AGAIN

**They ate their food with gladness and simplicity of heart,
praising God and having favor with all the people. And every day
the Lord added to them those who were being saved.**

ACTS 2:46–47

WE LOVE TO LOOK BACK to the early church as the model for
what we want to see happening in our own communities and fel-
lowships. But we will never fully understand the way the church
worked and multiplied, nor will we comprehend the power that
was available to them—*and to us*—if we miss these two points:

1. The church is based on the resurrection of Christ.

2. And it's designed to advance the kingdom of God.

In the last chapter we looked primarily at the first of these
themes—the church's declaration of victory over death. And now,
in this chapter, we'll talk about how this reality takes shape in the
experience of the church, how the life of the kingdom flows
through the lives of God's kingdom people.

This was already beginning in Jesus' final weeks before ascend-
ing to the Father, as he repeatedly came to his disciples and "presented Himself alive to them by many convincing proofs,
appearing to them during 40 days and speaking about the kingdom of God" (Acts 1:3).

To the resurrected Christ, kingdom teaching was his highest priority.

And the early church picked up on this right away.

The book of Acts, of course, tells their story. Yet in one sense, it's an open-ended story—a living drama that continues to this very day, still being written as God empowers and enlarges his church to fulfill his kingdom purpose.

Let's step inside and see what we can learn.

KINGDOM PRIORITIES

Among the many things we can observe from the Book of Acts and transpose into our own times as kingdom priorities are statements like these:

1. *The church proclaims the gospel.*

Most everyone in the early church was well aware that hundreds of years before—by virtue of Israel's disobedience—the Jews had been taken away captive into foreign lands. Yet now, because of the people's obedience to God's Word and his will, the church was being scattered by persecution into the remote corners of the earth. They were becoming his movable possessions, not by default but by desire.

Instead of rebelling against God, as their forefathers had done, the first-century believers embraced this uprooting as a necessary part of his plan. They were able to see that his kingdom can grow anywhere God's people are and that it often grows best just outside their comfort zones.

Therefore, as the Scripture says, "Those who were scattered went on their way proclaiming the message of good news" (Acts 8:4).

And it wasn't just the preachers who were doing it. Philip was a deacon, a layman selected as a servant to assist the apostles. But driven out of Jerusalem by the threat of torture and jail time, he left town not seeking a place to hide but a place to serve. The Spirit led him to Samaria, where he "proclaimed the good news about the kingdom of God and the name of Jesus Christ." And even though the kingdom of darkness was in full force there, as evidenced by the sorceries of Simon the magician, the kingdom of God prevailed and "both men and women were baptized" (Acts 8:12). Proclaiming the news of Christ's redemption should be the church's main priority in advancing the kingdom.

2. *The church plants other churches.*

The scattering of the Jerusalem believers also led to the planting of a church in Antioch (Acts 11:19–30). And before long, this church was led by the Spirit to give birth to other churches,[1] by sending Barnabas and an upstart convert named Saul of Tarsus into the neighboring regions (Acts 13:2–3).

This practice was and continues to be fundamental to the advance of God's kingdom. It's a task sufficiently large enough that throughout history churches have voluntarily organized themselves with other like-minded congregations in order to accomplish it. These denominational groupings are able to multiply a single church's individual efforts into one strong, aggressive, worldwide missions strategy. I believe this to be a natural progression of appropriate kingdom thinking—something we should generously fund, support, and participate in. But whatever we do, we should remember that at the heart of any authentic missions program is the establishment of healthy, local churches.

3. *The church shatters prejudice and unites people.*

We are told that when Barnabas first arrived in Antioch to see what the Lord was accomplishing there, he "saw the grace of God" in action (Acts 11:23). What did he really mean by this?

Well, we know that Antioch was one of the first places where new believers began preaching to the Greeks about Jesus, "and a large number who believed turned to the Lord" (v. 21). This barrier between Jews and Gentiles was indeed a formidable one that created friction among people on almost every level—racially, religiously, and socially. But to watch with one's own eyes as this "dividing wall of hostility" was being demolished by Christ's love and peace (Eph. 2:14), to see the radical changes that could take place when God's kingdom really rolled into town, was truly breathtaking.

Unfortunately today, in many of our churches, we are so focused on ourselves and our own constituencies that we fail either to experience or to show the world the uniting power of the gospel. Many churches function as if their only concern is for those already on the membership rolls, with no strategy or hunger in place to reach those who don't know Christ as King. Their small groups and Sunday schools have stagnated and lost their passion for thinking outside the normal, the easily attained, the readily available.

In contrast, the kingdom church should have a burning appetite and a real plan for reaching the world, for being willing to risk going to those outside the racial and socioeconomic makeup of our own neighborhoods—and not just because we want to notch converts and achieve success. We should love others so much that we *want* to have fellowship with them, to be united with them as fellow members of the family of God. We should be maintaining a global focus even inside our own communities, many of which are growing more international by the day.

4. *The church teaches sound doctrine.*

In the passage that is perhaps most descriptive of the early church—Acts 2:42–47—we can glean a lot of things. And among them is this clear portrayal of the believers being "devoted to the apostles' teaching" (v. 42). Some within today's church growth movement have suggested that we need to avoid doctrinal issues if we have any hope of reaching the modern-minded person. But this is as untrue as it is unbiblical. The effective, kingdom-focused church is deliberate and wholehearted about teaching the truths of the faith through its preaching and ministry.

5. *The church enjoys fellowship and builds relationships.*

Also found in the Acts 2 passage is a reference to the church being "together" and having "everything in common" (v. 44). In another verse, the Bible reports that "there was not a needy person among them" (Acts 4:34), for they were taking seriously their commitment to one another. This idea of fellowship as it was practiced in the early church was not just a potluck dinner they shared every once in a while. No, their fellowship was highly practical and continual. And still today the kingdom church is not a once-a-week phenomenon. It is a family of faith that enjoys one another's company and meets one another's needs. Wouldn't you love to be known as a "no-need" church?

6. *The church worships the living God.*

I'm talking about the kind of worship that is active and life-changing. For example, the idea of commissioning Barnabas and

Saul for their missionary journey came to the church at Antioch as they were "ministering to the Lord" (Acts 13:2), worshipping him with open, receptive hearts, truly seeking to conform themselves to his will. Even the reference to breaking bread "from house to house" (Acts 2:46) probably refers to the taking of the Lord's Supper and therefore speaks of the consistency and intimacy of their worship.

7. *The church experiences supernatural empowering.*

The church at Antioch was the first to be called "Christians" by the secular community—meaning "little Christs" or "imitators of Christ"—because their lifestyle was so radically infused by the unexplainable . . . except for the fact that they were in relationship with Jesus. But it wasn't just in Antioch that people were noticing a difference. The Acts 2 passage says that fear and awe were common reactions to what was happening in and through the lives of God's people.

All of the things we've been discussing in this chapter were coming together to produce amazing evangelistic fruit in the early church. Hundreds and thousands were receiving Christ and being baptized. The vibrant witness and visible distinction that characterized their daily lives were the talk of the town. And every sunrise brought the expectation that God would be doing even more through his kingdom people.

AND THEN WHAT?

It must have been incredibly exciting! And it can still be this exciting again—if we as a church will enter each day with our eyes trained on the kingdom, emptying ourselves of the desire to build our own kingdoms, making available to the Spirit of God a humble, obedient people to inspire and empower.

And as he does, we can expect our experience to be like that of the early church:

- They boldly and biblically proclaimed Jesus Christ.
- The Holy Spirit created a spontaneous, joyful response.
- Yet intense opposition resulted in increased persecution.

Paul could testify to this. When he arrived in Pisidian Antioch (Acts 13:13–52), he went to the synagogue and was asked if he had a word of exhortation for the people. His response, of course, was a bold declaration of the gospel—how "God brought the Savior, Jesus, to Israel" (v. 23). After a faithful retelling of Christ's life, death, and resurrection, he made clear "that through this man forgiveness of sins is being proclaimed to you, and everyone who believes in Him is justified from everything" (vv. 38–39).

As the Spirit planted this seed in the listeners' hearts, the people were stunned, wanting to hear more, begging "that these matters be presented to them the following Sabbath" (v. 42). When the day finally arrived, "almost the whole town assembled to hear the message of the Lord" (v. 44).

But like clockwork, this enthusiastic response also netted intense animosity. The Jews, "filled with jealousy and began to oppose what Paul was saying by insulting him" (v. 45), instigating enough persecution to drive Paul and Barnabas out of the district.

This scene has all the appearances of a great opportunity being choked and overpowered by its opposition into failure. Yet God, like his kingdom, always has the last word. And the last words of Acts 13 tell us that "the disciples were filled with joy and the Holy Spirit" (v. 52).

Yes, opposition is to be expected. The adversary doesn't give up his territory easily.

But because God is at work in his people, the kingdom *will* come.

Yes, But . . .

These were the experiences and lasting legacies of the early church, and they serve to remind us of what should still be most important to God's people, even this far removed from the first century.

Everything is about the kingdom, just as Paul demonstrated by continually "engaging in discussion and trying to persuade [others] about the things related to the kingdom of God" (Acts 19:8). Even in our last glimpse of him at the unfinished ending of the Book of Acts, he was awaiting trial in Rome, living in a rented house, "proclaiming the kingdom of God and teaching the things concerning the Lord Jesus Christ with full boldness and without hindrance" (Acts 28:31).

This is the heartbeat of the church—now as well as then.

We have not outgrown this heyday of kingdom advance. We continue to live in days that are ripe for reaching our neighborhoods and nation with the gospel of Jesus Christ, experiencing his kingdom fruit in our daily lives, sending and supporting missionaries around the globe, and praying for those who are embodying Christ to the unsaved people of the world.

We are fully able to embrace God's kingdom priorities as his community on earth: proclaiming Christ's redemption, establishing new churches, uniting diverse types of people, teaching sound doctrine, enjoying true fellowship, giving ourselves to worship, and expecting God to work among us.

But it takes more than wanting to. It takes more than wishing it could be so. It even takes more than our best efforts, our keenest planning, and our bulldog determination.

It takes Holy Spirit power.

And that's what I want to talk about in the next chapter.

- Compare your experience in churches today with the early church. What similarities/differences do you see?
- If churches have many of the same characteristics of the early church, are those characteristics evident in the lives of people who participate in churches today?
- Where do you see yourself in the church today? How does that affect who you are?

Chapter 28

HOLY SPIRIT POWER

But you will receive power when the Holy Spirit has come upon you, and you will be My witnesses in Jerusalem, in all Judea and Samaria, and to the ends of the earth.

ACTS 1:8

HOW DO WE MERE MORTALS dare think that we can advance the kingdom of God on earth? Since few of us ever hope to attain greatness in the eyes of the world, we just don't consider ourselves all that powerful or influential. It's overwhelming for most of us to think we could actually be involved in daily conversations and actions that will truly impact eternity.

But every Christian who lives with kingdom purpose can know true greatness. And this is why: "for thine is the power!" (see Matt. 6:13). *We can't,* but *he will!*

In truth this is the only way we will ever see lasting, spiritual fruit growing from the things we do or say. Any other approach is destined for a temporary shelf life and guaranteed insignificance. We must let God inspire and direct us if we are to perform his kingdom purposes. Genuine kingdom ministry requires supernatural empowering.

This strategic focus of kingdom activity radically changed in Acts 1:8. Up until then Jesus had been the kingdom of God in the flesh. So for those disciples who were on earth during Jesus' lifetime, the kingdom was *among* them (Luke 17:21). From Acts 1:8 on, however, the kingdom was *within* them. The emphasis of kingdom activity shifted from *him* to *them.*

So as Jesus said to his disciples, "You will receive power" and "you will be My witnesses," he wasn't leaving the matter open to discussion. Nor was he asking them to put forth their own effort in becoming effective spokespersons for his cause. Both their power and their witness were to be direct consequences of receiving the Holy Spirit.

And this is still vividly true today. Kingdom people are not given an option about being entrusted with God's power and his message. We are given instead the Holy Spirit, who produces all the necessary power within us to propel our witness.

He is God in us, enabling us to advance his kingdom and do his will.

With him inside we have everything we need.

PENTECOST

Pentecost was a traditional harvest festival known as the Feast of Weeks because it was celebrated fifty days (seven weeks) after Passover—in other words, a week of weeks. It was also called the "day of firstfruits" (Num. 28:26) because it marked the time when people began to bring the first and best of their harvest to the Lord. Every able-bodied man was expected to be present at the sanctuary to honor this important occurrence (Lev. 23:15–22).

When Pentecost rolled around on the year of Jesus' death—a few days, really, after his return to heaven—this religious observance had drawn Jews from all the surrounding countryside to

Jerusalem. Christ's followers were there too—"all together in one place" (Acts 2:1)—unsure and unsettled about the future that faced them with Jesus now gone. They were clinging to his instructions "not to leave Jerusalem," his command for them to "wait for the Father's promise" (Acts 1:4).

And God chose this moment in history to pour out the Holy Spirit on his people and give birth to his kingdom community.

Two powerful phenomena marked this event—"a violent rushing wind" and "tongues like flames of fire" (vv. 2–3). Both are Old Testament images. The *wind* represented God's power, and the *fire* his presence. Like the wind that animated the dry bones in Ezekiel's prophecy and the burning bush that alerted Moses to the holy presence of God, these two striking indicators energized an otherwise routine observance into something far beyond anything they could have expected.

Suddenly those who were gathered there from all the known nations of the world (v. 5) began hearing the good news of Jesus Christ in their own languages—a direct fulfillment of God's desire that his people proclaim the gospel to every tongue, tribe, and people group.

Those who were resistant to God's kingdom could only sneer and accuse the early disciples of being drunk. We know that when someone is drunk, his behavior and speech are controlled by the effect of the alcohol on his brain. I find it interesting that Paul exhorted the Ephesian church not to "get drunk with wine, which leads to reckless actions, but be filled with the Spirit" (Eph. 5:18). When we are indwelled and controlled by the Spirit of God, both our speech and behavior *will* be positively and powerfully influenced by his presence. They may call it being *drunk,* but we call it being delighted with God.

Peter, too, was amazed at what he was experiencing. In him we see the Holy Spirit in full operation.

This is the same man whose spiritual discernment had once been so weak, human, and limited that when Jesus had warned his disciples of his approaching death, Peter took him aside and began to rebuke him, "Oh no, Lord! This will never happen to You!" (Matt. 16:22). Yet now, filled with the Spirit at Pentecost, the Lord began helping him connect Old Testament prophecies with the things he was seeing.

This is the same man who a few weeks earlier couldn't stand up to a lowly servant girl, yet here we was, standing before the assembled masses, declaring God's truth with boldness and clarity.

Filled with kingdom power, he had become a kingdom witness.

And we are included in these blessings of Pentecost. We too are the sons and daughters, the young and the old, the slaves upon whom God has poured out his Spirit (vv. 17–18), filling us with power and the truth of his Word.

The moment we received Christ as our personal Savior, we were invaded by the life of the Spirit. As Paul made clear, "You, however, are not in the flesh, but in the Spirit, since the Spirit of God lives in you" (Rom. 8:9a). The Spirit enables us to address God as our Father and provides us with the internal testimony that "we are God's children" (Rom. 8:16). He baptizes (*immerses* or *integrates*) us all into "one body," so that we are "all made to drink of one Spirit" (1 Cor. 12:13).

No event subsequent to salvation is required for us to receive the full expression of God's Holy Spirit. We are only required to appropriate daily his infilling by emptying ourselves through prayer and confession and allowing him to consume more and more of us.

"For thine is the power."

THE POWER TO WITNESS

Throughout the Book of Acts, the Holy Spirit guided and empowered the bold advance of God's kingdom. The abundant response of three thousand souls at Pentecost was proof in itself of the fruitful work of the Spirit (Acts 2:41).

Later, when the disciples were thrown into jail for preaching about the resurrection, and when their accusers wanted to know the source of their power, "Peter was filled with the Holy Spirit" as he responded with bold assurance and unbridled truth (Acts. 4:8). His Spirit-empowered message was clear. He spoke under the authority of the name of Jesus. And as a result, when they observed "the boldness of Peter and John" and realized that they were "uneducated and untrained men, they were amazed and knew that they had been with Jesus" (v. 13). The authorities could threaten them, they could beat them, they could dangle over them the spectre of death, but they could not make them stop speaking about the things they had seen and heard (v. 18).

This can only be explained by the power of the Holy Spirit.

Nor can anything else explain:

- Philip being led away from revival in Samaria, out into the middle of a desert highway, where an Ethiopian man just happened to be traveling by and seeking the Lord in the scrolls of Isaiah's writings (Acts 8:26–39).

- Peter reluctantly going to the home of a Gentile named Cornelius, forcing the church to break free of its Jewish confines and open its arms to the enemy as friends (Acts 10).

- The Holy Spirit speaking to the church at Antioch and telling them to set apart Barnabas and Paul for the first missionary journey. The Spirit himself was the one who sent them out to take the message of hope to the nations of the world (Acts 13:1–4).

If it weren't for the Spirit of God empowering us to do so, we could no more take the gospel to the far corners of the world than we could take it to the corner of the street.

But with his life at work in us, the pressure is off. And the command to love our neighbor as we love ourselves emboldens us to share with them eternal life.

We have no reason to take the gospel to the corner of the street or the far corners of the world—except for this: we have been empowered by God's Spirit to do so.

THE FRUIT OF THE SPIRIT

The Spirit not only provides the power for witness, however. He also produces the fruit of holiness. We don't make ourselves pure and righteous before God in any other way. The Holy Spirit alone enables us to obey.

Paul says, for example, that in walking and living "by the Spirit," we will not "carry out the desire of the flesh" (Gal. 5:16). Sure, we still have this human nature to deal with. We face all kinds of Satan's tricks, deceits, and temptations. And part of us wants to go along with what he offers, consuming the blessings of God for ourselves.

But these fleshly desires are opposed to the desires of the Spirit—those desires which now dwell inside of us as a result of the Spirit's coming to live in us at salvation. He alone can convince us that those who live for themselves "will not inherit the kingdom of God" (Gal. 5:21), that the habitual and unrepentant practice of sin can only mean one thing: our lives are void of the Spirit.

But in submitting our will to his way—in surrendering the short-term glory of our kingdom for the eternal reward of the Father—the Spirit spontaneously produces in us "love, joy, peace, patience, kindness, goodness, faith, gentleness, self-control" (Gal. 5:22–23).

These are character traits we can't work up on our own. Oh, we may be able to dabble around the edges and display them at one time or another. But only the Spirit can make these a consistent, genuine, ongoing experience in our lives.

How do we let him do it, though?

We daily, continually surrender ourselves to his infilling. We know, for example, that we cannot totally fill a pitcher with water if it's partially filled with something else. Likewise, the Spirit cannot totally fill us if we are partially filled with sin. But "if we confess our sins, He is faithful and righteous to forgive us our sins and to cleanse us from all unrighteousness" (1 John 1:9). This is the way to be filled afresh with the Holy Sprit and power.

Think of it like this. View your body as if you were looking at a clear glass container, and imagine the unconfessed sin in your life as a corrosive element that has turned the clean water into a dark, gray sludge. As you confess your sins, get a mental image of all the pollution draining from the container until it is filled again with sparkling, clear water.

You may even want to confess your way through the body parts. For example, if you begin from the top down, you can start with the brain, confessing your evil thoughts. Then drain the eyes by confessing those sins that involve your sight. The ears represent the gossip or dirty jokes you've listened to, and the mouth represents the sins of speech. You can actually proceed down to the feet with this process in mind.

When you've finished confessing, picture the Holy Spirit cleansing the container so that it is pure once more. This time start from the bottom up, the same way a glass is filled. As you dedicate your feet and legs to him, which represent the places you'll be going throughout the day, picture them being filled with living water. Proceed back through each body part, dedicating all of them to the Lord and seeking his empowering.

Remember, God is searching for a people who will display his character. And he has given us his Holy Spirit to produce his character through us. He can, and he will.

THE GIFTS OF THE SPIRIT

In addition to empowering us to witness and inspiring us to holiness, the Spirit also energizes us with gifts of grace that enliven us for kingdom work—not to amaze or amuse us but to enable us to edify the church. Paul gave us the most succinct look at the function of the gifted church in Romans 12:1–8, reminding us of valuable truths like:

1. *God doesn't want our ability but our availability.* We all have something to offer the Father by serving him through his church. And he has declared that when we present our spiritual gifts to him in obedience to his will, they are "holy and pleasing" in his sight (v. 1).

2. *Using our gifts properly requires a renewed mind.* This enables us to see ourselves as God sees us—forgiven and empowered. Thus we will not be arrogant in our service but will have sound judgment. Those who boast about their role in serving God indicate that they are attempting to serve God through their own human ability. Similarly, those who whine that they have nothing of value to offer him neglect the clear teaching of Scripture and weaken the body.

3. *Every Christian is spiritually gifted.* Perhaps you've looked and looked, but you just can't seem to find yourself on any of the various spiritual gift lists in the New Testament. Don't despair! These lists were not intended to be comprehensive but only illustrative. God equips his people in every generation to accomplish his mission, through countless ways and opportunities. Look for those things God has enabled you to do which can help your church accomplish God's mission.

4. *The unity of the body is enhanced by diversity.* God didn't stamp his people out with a cookie cutter. You don't have to teach or sing or preach to be important to the work of your church. Do what God has gifted you to do.

5. *We need one another.* No one possesses *all* the gifts *all* by himself. This is by God's design, showing us that we are interdependent, that we only function best when we are functioning together. We will not accomplish God's purposes unless we all do

our part in the body of Christ. Your church is weaker when you don't serve according to your giftedness.

6. *Spiritual gifts have a singular purpose.* God has not given us these supernatural abilities to impress our friends or elevate ourselves. His sole desire in equipping us with gifts of grace and service is to build up the body of Christ. "So also you—since you are zealous in matters of the spirit, seek to excel in building up the church" (1 Cor. 14:12).

Yes, as we've seen in the last few chapters:

- The church is based on the resurrection of Christ.
- And it's designed to advance the kingdom of God.

But if we are to succeed at being part of this kingdom purpose, we must be empowered by the Holy Spirit.

And then . . . the world had better watch out!

- Where do you see God's power at work in the world today?
- If you were a "fruit" inspector, where would you find the best "fruit"?
- Which fruit of the Spirit do you think is most abundant in your life? Which fruit do you wish was more plentiful in your life?

Chapter 29

ONE EYE ON THE SKY

When the Son of Man comes in His glory, and all the angels with Him, then He will sit on the throne of His glory.

MATTHEW 25:31

AS A YOUNG LAD, I was always fascinated with the story of Robin Hood, amazed by his exploits and his ability with a bow and arrow. I remember as a kid trying to duplicate his feats . . . with little success.

But the plot running behind this familiar story was the delayed return of King Richard. In his absence evil men had taken control of the government and were squandering the resources of the kingdom, behaving as if he would never return. Robin Hood, on the other hand—through all of his remarkable adventures— was working from a totally different perspective. He was always bravely laboring in the light of the return of England's rightful king.

I'm sure you see the parallel.

Just as in the story of Robin Hood, we Christians labor for a King who is now physically absent from the earth. And—just like Robin Hood's contemporaries—many people today are squandering the King's resources, living as if he were never coming back.

But our King *will* return! His kingdom *is* coming! And if we hope to experience this kingdom in the midst of our daily lives, we must live in the light of this fundamental truth. We must live as if we really believe it.

His future return must matter to us today.

For to a timeless God, the final ingathering of the kingdom is as real and current now as it will be at some future point in human history. This is why we who serve him in this hour, in this kingdom moment, can live right now in the full victory and assurance of his eternal reality.

That's not to say that there isn't some mystery involved in his second coming. Even as long ago as the first century, Jesus' disciples were already wondering, "When will these things happen? And what is the sign of Your coming and the end of the age?" (Matt. 24:3).

There's always been a fascination about the end of time. Turbulent current events frequently trigger speculation about it, which inevitably prompts a new round of books attempting to understand the signs. But Jesus' response to his disciples' questions moved beyond speculation and focused on the certainty of his return—and the responsibilities of those who must wait patiently for his appearing.

He delivered his answer wrapped in five kingdom parables.

GET READY, STAY READY

The first brief parable illustrated the suddenness and unexpected nature of Jesus' coming.

His picture in this story was of a home owner who had suffered an unexpected robbery (Matt. 24:42–44). Obviously, Jesus said, if the man had known when the thief was coming, he would've been there waiting for him. He never would have allowed his house to be broken into if he'd had a little warning.

Jesus, of course, has given us ample warning to get ready for his soon return. He's not trying to trick us or outsmart us. We know that his delay is based on his own patient desire, on the beat of his kingdom heart—"not wanting any to perish, but all to come to repentance" (2 Pet. 3:9). Therefore, the exact timing of his return remains a mystery us.

So the only way to be ready for it is to stay ready for it.

When the Thessalonian believers became overanxious about the time of Christ's second coming, Paul told them they didn't need any additional information in order to be at peace with this. "For you yourselves know very well that the Day of the Lord will come just like a thief in the night" (1 Thess. 5:2). The believer's job is to "stay awake" (v. 6) and "encourage one another" (v. 11) with constant reminders that our hope is just around the corner and as sure as the sunrise.

So "get ready," Jesus said. Don't ignore his warning or put off your kingdom commitment for some later day that may never arrive. Today could be just as good a day as any other for our King to return, and we must be eager and watching, our eyes facing forward, not wanting to be caught by surprise but caught in the act of seeking the kingdom.

EXCEPTIONAL SERVICE

In the second parable Jesus addressed the issue of *our service to others* in light of his return. He used the imagery of a servant, one who obeys his master's wishes by tending to the needs of his fellow servants (Matt. 24:45–51).

While our King is absent, he has put us "in charge of his household"—entrusted with all of his possessions, which includes his other servants. So our business while waiting for his promised return is to make sure that those within our reach are loved and cared for, the way he would minister to them if he himself were here in physical form.

This is our pathway to blessing, Jesus said—not by seeking the best advantage for ourselves, not by occupying the majority of our prayer time with our own needs and wants, but by investing our time and resources in the lives of other people. This is what kingdom citizens do while they wait, resting in the full assurance of his bountiful reward.

But those who presume on God's patience and grace, who anticipate a long delay in his appearing and neglect the needs of others by chasing the selfish pursuits of sin, will suffer a certain judgment for their foolishness. Only those who are in relationship with the King, and who embody his name by showing compassion to others, show themselves to be kingdom people.

SUPPLIES ON HAND

The third parable teaches us *the wisdom of preparation.*

Jesus pictured a wedding scene, a special event that would have been familiar to all of his original hearers (Matt. 25:1–13). Weddings in Jesus' day were longer and more complex than our present-day observances. In the customs of his Jewish culture, the bridegroom and his friends would proceed from the groom's house, symbolically claiming the bride from her parents. The groom would then return home with her to celebrate in a grand wedding feast.

We don't know if the "virgins" in Jesus' parable were attendants of the bride, servants in the groom's home, or just invited guests. But we do know the wedding was an evening affair, complete with a torchlight procession as the maidens went out to escort the bridegroom.

But there was an unexpected delay in the festivities, and during the heavy hours of waiting, the maidens had fallen asleep—only to be awakened by a shout at midnight. "Here's the groom! Come out to meet him" (Matt. 25:6).

You know how the story goes from here. Five of the virgins hadn't foreseen the holdup. They were only prepared to join the party if it came off like they wanted, in just the way they expected it to occur. They wanted it to happen on their own terms and their own time line.

But as their lamps began to flicker from having to burn longer than they'd hoped—from having been asked to do more than they'd bargained for—they appealed to the others to give them some of their oil. But the wise maidens—the ones who had come prepared to march at the groom's command, the ones who understood whose day they had really come to celebrate—had only enough oil in reserve for themselves. So while the others were out looking for a merchant to buy oil from at midnight, the door was shut. The lock was bolted. The festivities were begun.

And the five "foolish ones" (v. 8) were left outside to deal forever with this stinging indictment: "I assure you, I do not know you" (v. 12).

When interpreting parables, we must always be careful not to over-allegorize the details. But we have many other biblical references (Isa. 54:4–5; Jer. 2:2; Matt. 9:15) to help convince us that the bridegroom is Jesus and that God had always referred to his people as his bride. Further, we easily see in the wedding feast a picture of the messianic banquet prophesied in Revelation 19:9, where those who are included are the ones who've been prepared through their personal relationship with the bridegroom.

So we're safe to draw a few logical conclusions:

1. *No one can rely on another's preparation.* We can't borrow oil from our parents' faith or our membership in a particular church.

2. *There is a "shut door" in God's timetable.* When the Lord returns, the door to the festival will be permanently closed. Realizing what's at stake, it would be foolish beyond comprehension to delay being ready or to hope in anything else.

3. *Entry is based on our relationship with the bridegroom.* The statement, "I do not know you," is in the perfect tense and can be translated, "I *have* not known you and do not *now* know you." It's not that the maidens were once known but were now rejected. It's not as if we can be biblically assured of our salvation and yet remain ever at risk of being left at the altar. Those who are excluded from fellowship with the kingdom family have never really been a part of it.

Those who fail to enter the kingdom will do so because of their own neglect.

WHERE THE MONEY GOES

Jesus' fourth parable dealt with *our need to invest in the kingdom.*

This story is probably even more familiar than the previous one—about a man who, before leaving on a long journey, entrusted three of his servants with differing amounts of *talents,* the currency of the day (Matt. 25:14–30).

Two of the servants, we all remember, invested the money and doubled their initial principal. The servant with the single talent, though, was afraid he might lose his master's money, so he buried it in the ground—failing to understand his master's purpose, fearfully substituting security for service.

This one who deemed the opportunity presented by his master as insignificant, as not worth messing with, actually ended up with less than he started, being stripped of even his one link to the master's grace and blessing. He simply didn't know who his master was. He had no understanding of his character.

But those who saw in their master's generosity a treasure to be invested in others and grown for his glory received as their reward his glowing affirmation, an enlarged opportunity to serve him, and the promise of sharing his lasting joy—the bread and butter of a kingdom person's desire.

Again, this gives us a lot to chew on in thinking about what our lives should be like in expectation of our Lord's return:

1. *Everything we own is an investment opportunity.* The things we do with the resources God has placed in our hands have eternal consequences. Our talents, our money, our time, our opportunities have all been earmarked for kingdom use.

2. *We each have significance as kingdom citizens.* The great value of the "talents" in this parable underlines the trust our King has placed in us. There are no insignificant members of Christ's body. Your life counts for more than you know!

3. *We are only responsible for what we've been given.* All of our earthly resources have been given to us "according to [our] own ability" (v. 15). Therefore, comparing our activity or assignment with someone else's is totally irrelevant. Isn't it wonderful that God deals with us as individuals, understanding perfectly our circumstances and personalities? We must be productive with what we've received and not worry about what we lack.

4. *Our lives have a future-accountability component.* God is constantly offering us kingdom opportunities. This is why we must daily, regularly pray, "Your kingdom come" (Matt. 6:10), asking the Father to show us what he wants us to do, keeping ourselves in a state of continual availability.

5. *Avoiding sin is only half the battle.* The guy with the one talent may have felt like he was doing something noble by not making a risky mistake with his money. But being content with not doing wrong will keep us from enjoying the freedom and adventure of serving Christ with head-on abandon.

6. *The Father's reward is always enough.* His affirmation is sufficient reward. And life with him, enjoying the radiance of his smile and presence, is all we could ever want.

The bottom line of this parable is this: are you *spending* your life or *investing* it?

UNTIL THE END

Even more familiar than any of the others, perhaps, is Jesus' fifth parable, the sheep and the goats (Matt. 25:31–46), which identifies *the ongoing activities of kingdom citizens.*

In Jesus' day flocks of sheep and goats were often mixed together as one in the same pasture. On market day, however, as the animals were being driven through a narrow chute, a shepherd would swing open a gate to the right or the left, and the goats and sheep that had once grazed together in the field would now be separated forever.

This is our experience, too. The saved and the unsaved often live right next door to one another, each consuming the resources of the one King of creation. But at the final reckoning, there will be an absolute and eternal separation of the two.

Some have suggested that this picture of judgment teaches a *works* salvation. Not so! The criterion God will use in judging us is not the measure of our philanthropy, but the reality of our relationship to him—as evidenced by the fruit we have borne in serving both him and our fellowman.

It's like what Jesus told his disciples back in Matthew 10, when he commissioned them to go out to the neighboring towns preaching the kingdom of God. He sent them without provision, promising that those who responded to their message would welcome them into their homes. "The one who welcomes you welcomes Me, and the one who welcomes Me welcomes Him who sent Me" (v. 40). It wasn't the people's warm hospitality that earned them the blessing of God. Their hospitality was the proof that they had received Christ's message in their hearts. Repentance and belief opened the door, and their changed lifestyle simply followed their confession home.

And we are to be on both sides of this equation:

1. *We are to be warning the world of coming judgment,* fully aware that hell has been "prepared for the Devil and his angels" (Matt. 25:41), not for men created in the image of God. Our hearts must beat and our feet must follow in the direction of those

who need to hear this message of hope. Judgment is coming, and our business is urgent.

2. *We are to be meeting human needs in Jesus' name,* showing both the saved and the unsaved alike that our kingdom is real and its people are genuine, that our King is alive and he lives and breathes in us. These truths will pour forth through us in a hundred thousand ways, many of which will humble us beyond measure and muddy our hands with the filth and inconvenience of kingdom service. But our reward will be the Father's pat on our shoulder and the certainty of our forever life with him.

We do it for him. And oh, what he does for us!

Our king is coming. And the "good news of the kingdom" must be "proclaimed in all the world as a testimony to all nations. And then the end will come" (Matt. 24:14).

Then we'll take our place with the redeemed of all the ages. We'll rest our weary feet at the foot of Christ's glorious throne. We'll continue to worship and serve him, only now without the hindrance of nagging temptations or the drag of human fatigue.

But until then, we'll keep one eye on the sky . . . because his coming is already one day closer than it was just yesterday.

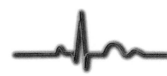

- *Domestic box-office receipts topped $9 billion in 2002.*
- *In 2000 Easter candy sales were expected to exceed $1.8 billion.*
- *In 2000 Americans spent $13 billion a year on chocolate.*

- *In 1999 overseas ministries income to more than 600 agencies, including denomination, interdenominational, and independent agencies was $2.9 billion. (Source:* http://emptytomb.org/lifestylestat.html, 12/16/2003)
- What do statistics reveal about where people invest their money?
- Describe a good "kingdom" investment.
- What kingdom investments have you made?

Chapter 30

FOREVER IN A DAY

**Therefore, since we are receiving a kingdom that cannot be
shaken, let us hold on to grace. By it, we may serve God
acceptably, with reverence and awe.**

HEBREWS 12:28

WE'VE COVERED THOUSANDS of years and dozens of important ideas since we first began this book together. We've wandered from one corner of the Bible to the next, traveling cross-country in our pursuit of the kingdom in all of its eternal reality.

But all this traveling in faraway lands and time zones has led us to the threshold of another new day. The kingdom—as huge and historic as it may be—has a practical way of beating a path to our door and settling down in our dens and living rooms, remaining as powerful and relevant at noon in a fast-food restaurant as it was on a Bible-lined page from the life of Moses or Elijah or John the Baptist.

God's kingdom has invaded the ordinary sights and sounds of our average day. It has stopped over the place where we swing by for coffee in the mornings. It has nestled into bed where we read our children stories at night or in the car where we talk homework and make plans and share our hopes for the summer. It has made itself at home in manufacturing plants and on playgrounds, over lunch and after dinner, in paneled boardrooms where we'd think the main topics of business were marketing plans and growth strategies.

The kingdom is here. It is now. And it's bigger than anything in this world that likes to think of itself as important.

The kingdom has brought meaning to our lives, cohesion to our thoughts, unfailing purpose to our dreams.

It has brought forever into this very day.

A HISTORY OF REDEMPTION

Real quickly—because we've seen so much over the past thirty chapters—let's take one more good flyover of the kingdom's life and purpose.

We need to remember, for example, that *the kingdom is God the Creator's rightful rule over all the earth and its people.* As the psalmist declared, "May he rule from sea to sea and from the Euphrates to the ends of the earth. . . . And let all kings bow down to him, all nations serve him" (Ps. 72:8, 11).

But although all things are subject to him, and will one day be visibly seen as such, *this is not yet the case on earth.* Satan has led a rebellion within God's kingdom, and God in his sovereign power and plan has allowed him temporary reign as the prince of the world (Eph. 2:2). Yes, "we know that we are of God" and have been redeemed from Satan's dominion by the blood of Christ, but "the whole world is under the sway of the evil one" (1 John 5:19). Therefore, we can easily spot the source of the world's pain, suffering, and death—what Paul speaks of as all creation "groaning together with labor pains" until Satan's short-term rule is ended forever (Rom. 8:22).

But in real historical time, and in response to Satan's rebellion, *God selected the people of Israel to redeem for his own.* He was seeking a nation that would embrace his mission to the nations, embody his name and character, and obey his Word the first time, without needing any other proof but his love for them. He promised to bless this people in order that all the nations of the earth might be drawn to him.

But Israel's willful disobedience led to discipline, disappointment, and ultimate defeat in terms of their kingdom task. They saw God's blessings as privileges to be consumed rather than treasures to be conveyed.

So through the prophets, *God promised to send a mighty Redeemer* who would claim a faithful remnant of this people into one, new messianic community. This coming King would sit on the throne of his father David forever, fulfilling God's covenant promise.

The fulfillment of this promise was accomplished by the costly gift of God's own Son. When Jesus declared that the kingdom of heaven was at hand, the earthly conflict with the devil reached a new level of immediate intensity. By his repeated practice of casting out demons, Jesus revealed one visibly convincing sign that Satan's kingdom was destined to fall. As Christ said, "If I drive out demons by the finger of God, then the kingdom of God has come to you" (Luke 11:20).

Surprisingly, the King's ultimate victory occurred with the most unlikely of coronations—his own death. But rather than asking his Father to save him from this painful humiliation, Jesus prayed that through his death the Father would glorify his own name. *So where Israel had failed in reflecting the Father's name, his obedient Son would not.* When God thundered his applause from heaven—"I have glorified [My name], and I will glorify it again" (John 12:28–29)—Jesus declared, "Now is the judgment of the world. Now the ruler of this world will be cast out. As for Me, if I am lifted up from the earth I will draw all people to Myself" (John 12:31–32).

The resurrection of Jesus was the conclusive declaration that the Son was victorious. He had gone to the very stronghold of the enemy and had emerged triumphant, "established as the powerful Son of God by the resurrection from the dead" (Rom. 1:4a). At that very moment *Satan's days on earth were numbered. He had been defeated! But he was not yet banished from the earth.* He is still allowed for a short while to prowl around "like a roaring lion, looking for anyone he can devour" (1 Pet. 5:8). Since his ultimate weapon—the power of death—has been majestically overcome, he must now resort to deceit and deception, attempting to thwart the advance of the kingdom.

Even now, however—while not visible to our earthly eyes— *Christ rules as King from his royal position in the Father's presence.* "This man, after offering one sacrifice for sins forever, sat down at the right hand of God. He is now waiting until His enemies are made His footstool" (Heb. 10:12–13).

The sovereign Lord, the King of glory, is directing all of history toward one event—the judgment of the nations and the full and visible establishment of his kingdom. *He works now through his church, to whom he has given the keys of the kingdom, the message of his salvation and redemption.* We are the people whom God has commissioned to reflect his character, obey his Word, and take his good news to the nations, showing people how to align themselves with God's rule and reign. Wherever and whenever his reign is established, Satan—the defeated one—must retreat.

In order to carry out this God-sized task, *the church has been fully empowered by Christ's Spirit,* which dwells within us as believers. The Father has "put everything under [Jesus'] feet and appointed Him as head over everything for the church, which is His body, the fullness of the One who fills all things in every way" (Eph. 1:22–23). Take heart, then! The church—*your church*—is fully empowered by God's Spirit to accomplish God's kingdom advance.

This is the essence of God's kingdom story.

COME, LORD JESUS

But his story is far from over.

We live now in the overlap of the ages that theologians call the "already/not yet." We are already experiencing kingdom empowering as believers in Christ, but we are still looking forward to a future brand of kingdom fullness. We have a taste, but it has only whetted our appetite for more, compelling us to extend his kingdom by sharing the gospel, planting new believers in thriving churches, and teaching modern-day disciples to obey the King.

Every day we live with this forever reality burning inside of us. We set off into each morning with the Hope of the world communicating his truth to us through his Word and by his Spirit. We enter every personal encounter by recognizing the possibility that we are staring a kingdom opportunity in the face.

We are filled with a joy that has transformed flesh and bone into salt and light.

For he is coming! Our King is coming—"One like the Son of Man, dressed in a long robe, and with a gold sash wrapped around His chest. His head and hair . . . white like wool—white as snow, His eyes like a fiery flame, His feet like fine bronze fired in a furnace, and His voice like the sound of cascading waters." He is "the First and the Last, and the Living One. I was dead, but look—I am alive forever and ever, and I hold the keys of death and Hades" (Rev. 1:13–15, 17–18).

Those who sit around his throne day and night "never stop, saying: Holy, holy, holy, Lord God, the Almighty, who was, who is, and who is coming" (Rev. 4:8b). They are joined in praise by the twenty-four elders, who cast their crowns before the throne and cry out in worship, "Our Lord and God, You are worthy to receive glory and honor and power, because You have created all things, and because of Your will they exist and were created" (Rev. 4:11).

He is the only one worthy to take the book from the Father's hand—"worthy to take the scroll and to open its seals; because You were slaughtered, and You redeemed people for God by Your blood from every tribe and language and people and nation. You made them a kingdom and priests to our God, and they will reign on the earth" (Rev. 5:9–10).

We can almost see him. Even today we can almost make out the glorious features of his face, counting ourselves among the myriads—that great throng comprised of "every creature in heaven, on earth, under the earth, on the sea, and everything in them" (Rev. 5:13), who gather around his throne in awe and reverence.

Stop where you are and worship! The King is coming!

Oh, how I wish I could tell you that in this mighty, kingdom culmination moment, everyone will join in the songs of praise. But this is sadly untrue. Once the sixth seal is broken, a great earthquake will occur, and the sun will turn "black like sackcloth." The entire moon will become "like blood," and the stars of heaven will fall to the earth "as a fig tree drops its unripe figs when shaken by a high wind." The sky will separate "like a scroll being rolled up," and every mountain and island will be "moved from its place" (Rev. 6:12–14).

"Then the kings of the earth, the nobles, the military commanders, the rich, the powerful, and every slave and free person" will rush in panic toward impossible places of safety, saying to the mountains and rocks, "Fall on us and hide us from the face of the One seated on the throne and from the wrath of the Lamb" (Rev. 6:15–16). Those who have rejected the King on earth will not be able to stand before him in praise.

But even while the final battle is progressing, before the enemy can surrender in shame, the seventh angel will declare that "the kingdom of the world has become the kingdom of our Lord and of His Messiah, and He will reign forever and ever!" (Rev. 11:15).

The great dragon and his angels, not strong enough to contend with the God of all creation, will be hurled to the earth. And again a loud voice from heaven will proclaim, "The salvation and the power and the kingdom of our God and the authority of His Messiah have now come, because the accuser of our brothers has been thrown out: the one who accuses them before our God day and night. They conquered him by the blood of the Lamb"—yes, the shed blood of Christ—but also "by the word of their testimony, for they did not love their lives in the face of death" (Rev. 12:10–11).

HIS KINGDOM NEVER FAILS

And so, here we stand—on this day, in this year—with the option of "loving our lives" being dangled by the devil before us, the road we've so often taken by ignoring the stirring of the Spirit within us and keeping his kingdom reality to ourselves.

Kingdom living does indeed come "in the face of death"—in the death of our pride, in the death of our sin, our greed, our fears, our selfish wants and wishes. It will cost us our desire to be left alone, our tight rein over our schedule of entertainment, our discomfort with anything more than hit-and-miss, here-and-there, cut-and-dried Christianity.

But it will change us. It will make us read these Revelation verses with a new appetite for holiness, with the fresh air of genuine gratitude, with the deep-seated assurance that our souls have been bought and paid for at the cost of Christ's blood.

We will want to be like him. We will want to be with him. We will want to be among his people in kingdom community and with every person we can to tell the good news.

We are living in kingdom days, alive as God's kingdom people.

Nothing is more important.

Nothing holds more promise.

And nothing can stop us now.

We are children of the King!

- What earthly kingdoms have come and gone in your lifetime?
- How does it make you feel that God's kingdom will stand forever and can never be shaken?

- How has God's grace been evident in your life?
- Are you pleased with your current level of service to God? Why/Why not?
- In awe and reverence, what will you seek to change, by God's grace, in your worship and service in his kingdom?

EPILOGUE

The good news of the kingdom will be proclaimed in all the world as a testimony to all nations and then the end will come.

MATTHEW 24:14

IT IS MY PRAYER that this book has had as profound an impact on your life as it has on mine. Perhaps you have been pondering what you should do now, as a result of investing so much of your time in reading and studying the matchless kingdom of God.

I would encourage you to start by reading again the Gospels, paying particular attention to the parables of the kingdom, reading them with your eyes open to the pervasive kingdom language and priorities in Jesus' teaching.

But it's not enough just to read the Word. James tells us we must *do* the Word. "Because if anyone is a hearer of the word and not a doer, he is like a man looking at his own face in a mirror; for he looks at himself, goes away, and right away forgets what kind of man he was. But the one who looks intently into the perfect law of freedom and perseveres in it, and is not a forgetful hearer but a doer who acts—this person will be blessed in what he does" (James 1:23–25).

If we lay this book aside with the simple conclusion that it contains some interesting ideas, we'll not only prove to be merely "hearers" of the Word, but we'll fail to confront honestly several important questions and establish a strategy to allow God to change and bless us:

Am I a kingdom person?

To answer this question at its most fundamental level, you must first deal honestly with your spiritual status. Are you a child of God? Have you been born again? If not, would you receive him as your Savior and Lord right now?

God created you in his image with the goal that you might know him as Father and live with him forever. "For God loved the world in this way: He gave His only Son, so that everyone who believes in Him will not perish but have eternal life" (John 3:16).

The only thing that separates you from God is your sin. "For all have sinned and fall short of the glory of God" (Rom. 3:23), and "the wages of sin is death" (Rom. 6:23). This verse refers to spiritual death which—if not resolved before *physical* death—will result in your separation from holy God for all eternity.

The solution to your sin problem is found in the second half of the verse I just mentioned: "For the wages of sin is death, but the gift of God is eternal life in Christ Jesus our Lord" (Rom. 6:23). Jesus died for your sins that he might personally "bring you to God" (1 Pet. 3:18). This is why the apostle John could declare, "To all who did receive Him, He gave them the right to be children of God, to those who believe in His name" (John 1:12).

I believe with all my heart that you want to become a child of God. So first you must agree with God about your sin problem, committing that you will turn away from your sin. "Repent . . . and be baptized, each of you, in the name of Jesus the Messiah for the forgiveness of your sins" (Acts 2:38). This repentance is accompanied by conviction and confession. "If you confess with your mouth, 'Jesus is Lord,' and believe in your heart that God raised Him from the dead, you will be saved" (Rom. 10:9).

Confess this to God, then talk to him in prayer. Here is a simple guide to help you:

"God, I admit that I'm a sinner. But this day I turn from my sin to follow you. I believe that you sent Jesus, who died on the cross and rose from the dead, paying the penalty of my sin. I receive your gift of forgiveness and eternal life. In Jesus' name I pray. Amen."

If you sincerely prayed that prayer, you are a child of God. You'll want to share this good news with a friend. If you have a friend or relative who is a Christian, start by telling him or her.

You'll also want to find a good church home where you can be nurtured by the teaching of God's Word. In terms of your Christian life, you are like a newborn infant. So "like newborn infants, desire the unadulterated spiritual milk, so that you may grow by it in your salvation" (1 Pet. 2:2). Make sure that you find a church that believes the Bible to be the authoritative Word of God and teaches it as truth. Don't be afraid to ask the pastor about his conviction concerning Scripture.

If you are certain that you are already a believer, you must still answer this question:

Am I a kingdom person?

Are you committed to spreading the gospel of the kingdom? Do your calendar and checkbook reflect kingdom priorities? If you are a parent, are you helping your children develop a kingdom focus? What would have to change in your life for you to be a kingdom person? What changes are you prepared to make . . . beginning today?

I am aware that many church groups may be studying this book with the desire to become more effective instruments in terms of kingdom activity. Then you should ponder *this* question:

Are we a kingdom church?

What would a kingdom-focused church look like? Does your church budget reflect God's passion to reach Jerusalem, Judea, Samaria, and the uttermost parts of the world? What are you doing to reach your Jerusalem? Do you have an evangelism strategy? Are you teaching people how to share their faith? Are you impacting the culture of your community? Are you salt and light? What things can you do to become salt and light as a church? Are you helping to nurture kingdom-focused families?

Please don't be discouraged if you think that you or your church cannot say that you're kingdom-focused. The bigger question is:

Do you want to be?

Once you know where you are and where you want to go, the Spirit will give you clear guidance. I promise, if this is your heart's desire and passion, you are about to embark on a wonderful kingdom journey.

I am praying for you. And I believe God will empower kingdom growth through us as we serve him together.

NOTES

CHAPTER 1, KINGDOM MOMENTS

1. James S. Stewart, *The Life and Teaching of Jesus Christ* (Nashville: Abingdon Press, 1947), 47.

CHAPTER 3, I WILL IF YOU WILL

1. If you would like to read more about the concept of covenant, you will find the article by Steven B. Cowan in the *Holman Bible Dictionary* to be most helpful (Nashville: Holman Bible Publishers, 1998), 355–59.

CHAPTER 4, A MOVABLE POSSESSION

1. John I. Durham, *Exodus,* Word Bible Commentary (Waco, Tex.: Word Books, 1987), 262.

2. Walter C. Kaiser Jr., *Mission in the Old Testament* (Grand Rapids, Mich.: Baker, 2000), 22.

3. Durham, *Exodus,* 262.

4. Kaiser, *Mission in the Old Testament,* 22.

CHAPTER 5, ENTRUSTED WITH GREATNESS

1. Durham, *Exodus,* 263.

2. Kaiser, *Mission in the Old Testament,* 23.

3. James Leo Garrett Jr., *New Testament Studies* (Waco, Tex.: Markham Press Fund, 1975), 141.

CHAPTER 6, SEE THE DIFFERENCE?

1. If you desire to know more about the name Jehovah Mekadesh, you should read chapter 9, *The Names of God,* by Ken Hemphill (Nashville: Broadman & Holman, 2001).

CHAPTER 7, KNOWN BY HIS NAME

1. J. A. Thompson, *Chronicles,* New American Commentary (Nashville: Broadman & Holman, 1994), 147.

CHAPTER 9, WHEN GOD'S PEOPLE QUIT CARING

1. For a more complete discussion of this period in Israel's history, see John Bright, *The Kingdom of God* (New York: Abingdon Press, 1953).

2. Daniel L. Block, *Ezekiel,* New American Commentary (Nashville: Broadman & Holman, 1994), 347–48.

CHAPTER 12, STARTING FRESH

1. Bright, *The Kingdom of God.*

2. Ibid., 94.

3. Hemphill, *The Names of God,* 153.

CHAPTER 13, THE KING IS COMING

1. For more information on the intertestamental period, see the article by Clayton Harrop in the *Holman Bible Dictionary* (Nashville: Holman Bible Publishers, 1998), 829–34.

2. These last two observations are from R. T. France, *Matthew,* Tyndale New Testament Commentaries (Grand Rapids, Mich.: William B. Eerdmans Publishing Company, 1985), 71.

3. Ibid., 45–46.

CHAPTER 16, GETTING HUNGRY?

1. David S. Dockery and David E. Garland, *Seeking the Kingdom* (Wheaton: Harold Shaw Publishers, 1992), 24.

CHAPTER 18, POINTS OF CONTACT

1. Dockery and Garland, *Seeking the Kingdom,* 36.

CHAPTER 19, ABOVE AND BEYOND

1. Warren W. Wiersbe, *Be Loyal* (Wheaton, Ill.: Victor Books, 1985), 35.

CHAPTER 20, WHERE'S MY REWARD?

1. G. Campbell Morgan, *The Gospel According to Matthew* (New York: Fleming H. Revell Company, 1929), 59.

2. Ibid., 60.

3. Jill Morgan, *A Man of the Word: The Life of G. Campbell Morgan* (New York: Fleming H. Revell Company, 1951), 59–60.

CHAPTER 21, KINGDOM PRAYER

1. I can only briefly summarize this prayer in the present work, but if your appetite has been whetted to know more, I recommend that you read my book, *The Prayer of Jesus* (Nashville: Broadman & Holman, 2001). Your church may also find the video study by the same name, produced by LifeWay Church Resources, to be a good follow-up to *Empowering Kingdom Growth.*

CHAPTER 26, GATE CRASHERS

1. Morgan, *The Gospel According to Matthew,* 215.

CHAPTER 27, ACTS ALL OVER AGAIN

1. If you are interested in learning more about the kingdom principles taught by the church at Antioch, you might find my book *The Antioch Effect* to be a helpful resource (Nashville: Broadman & Holman, 1994).

A 40 DAY EXPERIENCE

EKG

THE HEARTBEAT OF GOD

Empowering Kingdom Growth: The Heartbeat of God (B&H). This life-changing book about the meaning and power of God's kingdom is the basis for *A 40 Day Experience: EKG*. Ken Hemphill, whose impact has been felt as an author, pastor, and seminary president, explains how God's deep passion for us gives us the key to a life with eternal purpose and meaning.

ISBN 0-8054-3147-0

A 40 Day Experience: EKG member book is the small-group resource based on the life-changing message of *Empowering Kingdom Growth: The Heartbeat of God* (B&H) by Ken Hemphill. Seven small-group sessions and the daily devotions in between will help change your perspective and no doubt change your life.

ISBN 0-6331-9758-0

A 40 Day Experience: EKG Leader's Kit helps pastors and small-group leaders facilitate this 40 Day Experience. Each kit contains the *Empowering Kingdom Growth: The Heartbeat of God* (B&H) hardback, *A 40 Day Experience: EKG* member book, an *EKG* small-group DVD featuring the author, and a CD-ROM with an administrative guide, sermon outlines, and other helps.

ISBN 0-6331-9759-9

A 40 Day Experience: EKG resources are available at your local **LifeWay Christian Store**, online at **www.lifeway.com**, or by calling **800.458.2772**